Beaux-Arts Architecture in

Photographs by Edmund V. Gillon, Jr.

New York

A PHOTOGRAPHIC GUIDE

Text by Henry Hope Reed • DOVER PUBLICATIONS, INC., New York

HENRY HOPE REED, President, Classical America
EDITOR: The Classical America Series in Art and Architecture.
AUTHOR: *The Golden City; The New York Public Library: Its Architecture and Decoration; Rockefeller New York; American Skyline* (with Christopher Tunnard); *Central Park: A History and a Guide* (with Sophia Duckworth).

Copyright © 1988 by Dover Publications, Inc.
All rights reserved under Pan American and International
Copyright Conventions.

Published in Canada by General Publishing Company, Ltd.,
30 Lesmill Road, Don Mills, Toronto, Ontario.
Published in the United Kingdom by Constable and Company, Ltd.,
3 The Lanchesters, 162–164 Fulham Palace Road, London W6 9ER.

Beaux-Arts Architecture in New York: A Photographic Guide is a
new work, first published by Dover Publications, Inc., in 1988.
The diagrams on pages 85 and 86 are reproduced from
Illustrated Dictionary of Historic Architecture,
edited by Cyril M. Harris (Dover, ISBN 0-486-24444-X).

Manufactured in the United States of America
Dover Publications, Inc.
31 East 2nd Street
Mineola, N.Y. 11501

Library of Congress Cataloging-in-Publication Data

Gillon, Edmund Vincent.
Beaux-arts architecture in New York.

1. Eclecticism in architecture—New York (N.Y.)—Guide-books.
2. Architecture, Modern—19th century—New York (N.Y.)—Guide-books.
3. Architecture, Modern—20th century—New York (N.Y.)—Guide-books.
4. New York (N.Y.)—Buildings, structures, etc.—Guide-books.
I. Reed, Henry Hope. II. Title.
NA735.N5G55 1988   720'.9747'1   88-16120
ISBN 0-486-25698-7 (pbk.)

CONTENTS

v

INTRODUCTION

Beaux-Arts . . . How the phrase rings! It conveys a larger outlook, a willingness to see the world embellished, a range of knowledge in the arts embodied in the respect for our past, a certain sophistication to make use of the best.

Although the phrase is nothing more than the French for "fine arts," it has come to identify not a style, but a particular manner of execution and finish, especially in architecture, and today we accept it as primarily identifying the more outstanding monuments and buildings constructed between 1880 and 1930, a period, in its time, called the American Renaissance. "Beaux-Arts" is part of our Progressive Era, the City Beautiful Movement in civic design and city planning, the Edwardian Era, the Belle Epoque, the era of the grand luxury hotel—a building type which, in a way, evokes the phrase. The Ritz Hotels in London and Paris come to mind and, in New York, the Hotel St. Regis. As it so happens, the three famous hotels were designed by men who went to the Ecole des Beaux-Arts.

The phrase also had (and not so long ago) a pejorative connotation. It was "Bozarts" and, in print, the mocking variation would be accompanied by a cartoon of a top-hatted Frenchman sporting a spiky moustache and a spiky beard. The mockers were bored with hearing about the wonders of the famous Ecole, but it was the name of the school that gave the phrase its currency and identified it with architecture.

What was the Ecole Nationale Supérieure des Beaux-Arts? It was nothing more than the state school, located in Paris, for the training of painters, sculptors, architects and medallists. It consisted of ateliers (studios) headed by eminent professionals. The French government provided the facilities, which included a large library, a collection of casts (most of ancient sculpture and architectural ornament), copies of great murals (such as some of those of Michelangelo's ceiling in the Sistine Chapel). To enter, the aspirant had to pass examinations and show examples of work revealing some evidence of incipient talent. Instruction and discipline were provided by the students themselves under the guidance of a professional. It was, basically, an adaptation of the artist's studio or architect's apprentice system to the exigencies of the schoolroom. The result of the effort to achieve quality in training was that, by the time of the Second Empire, the Ecole had become the great training ground for the fine arts in Europe.

And the Americans? They had turned to Paris for instruction in the arts as early as the Napoleonic Era, when John Vanderlyn was sent there by Aaron Burr. In time Paris was to supplant London and Rome and outdistance Antwerp, Munich and Düsseldorf as the training ground for those who would be artists. In architecture, the first American was Richard Morris Hunt; we have this on no less an authority than Charles Follen McKim. He was at the Ecole from 1845 to 1853 in the atelier of Hector Lefuel, the designer of the new wings of the Louvre. Hunt even worked in Lefuel's office, and he is credited with that part of the palace known as the Pavillon de la Bibliothèque.

Henry Hobson Richardson, who later became the well-known Boston architect, was probably the next to go; that was in the 1860s. During these years, the gaudy decades of the Second Empire, Americans formed one of the larger foreign colonies in Paris. While their presence had no influence in bringing students to the Ecole, they did underscore the role of the city as a major port of call for the traveling American. In all probability, the most conspicuous American element was in the painting and sculpture ateliers in the 1870s; by the 1890s it had been surpassed by the number in the architectural ateliers. In the 1890s, Americans made up the largest foreign contingent in the Ecole studying architecture.

While it is true that the Paris-trained men were to be found among painters and sculptors, notably in the instances of Edwin Howland Blashfield, Kenyon Cox and Augustus Saint-Gaudens, they dominated in architecture. Through their professional distinction and influence, architectural training in the United States came to be modeled on that of the Ecole. The first atelier in the Beaux-Arts format was that of Hunt in 1857 held in the old Gothic building of New York University on the east side of Washington Square. From Hunt's atelier descended the nation's architecture schools, the first one being formed at the Massachusetts Institute of Technology in 1868 by William R. Ware, a pupil of Hunt best known as the author of *The American Vignola.*

This is not the place to dwell on the teaching of the Ecole. Rather an attempt should be made to examine the common thread that links the work of the men (and, later, of the women) trained there and those who came out of its American offshoots. For the "Beaux-Arts," to repeat, is not a style. The training encouraged the eclectic, although the emphasis was on the Classical. Whitney Warren, who went to the Ecole, ateliers of Daumet, Girault and Esquié, could produce the Classical Grand Central Terminal and the Flamboyant Gothic chapel in Green-Wood Cemetery. Richard Morris Hunt executed the Romanesque mausoleum of the Vanderbilt family in the Moravian Cemetery on Staten Island and the great central front of the Metropolitan Museum of Art. Let us not forget that the Statue of Liberty and its high base are the work of Paris-trained men, as is Rockefeller Center.

At the Ecole the first and most important step in design was the plan. The facade was to follow on the plan; there was to be no "false front." This approach could be applied to any style. Another very important aspect of the training, and it is surely the element that gave the Beaux-Arts its cachet, was the fact that the student was made to design palaces, although they might take the form of a bank, a central building for a spa, an ambassador's residence and chancellery. The emphasis was on large projects. This was notably true of the schemes submitted in the competition for the Grand Prix de Rome, the Ecole's highest award, the climax of the school training. Although restricted to Frenchmen—the winner going to the French Academy in Rome for several years—the prize inevitably gave direction to the curriculum. As competitors for the Prix had to turn to fellow students in rendering the final presentation—the elevations and plans were huge— Americans, although excluded from the competition, would assist their French colleagues in the detailing.

In the palace concept there was always plenty of room for murals and sculpture, especially sculptured ornament. This explains why the label Beaux-Arts is often pinned to an elaborately decorated Classical facade. This same palace concept conferred prestige on projects that induced artists to create monumental works to adorn them, such as at Grand Central Terminal and the New York Public Library.

One of the more conspicuous results of the Beaux-Arts training was the skill many of its graduates had in making renderings, for it was very important in conveying what a future building would look like. The technique is known as India-ink wash rendering; there is nothing to equal it in depicting a facade or a detail. Above and beyond their utilitarian purpose, they were beautiful drawings.

With all the training came a knowledge and an understanding of the art of architecture. The consequence was that, for all the influence of the Ecole, Americans rarely bowed to the work of their French colleagues. They drew freely on Europe's heritage, from the great Roman and Renaissance precedents up to the eighteenth century. For most of them, in drawing on the past, the goal was always beauty—not originality. As Cass Gilbert said, "aim for beauty; originality will take care of itself."

Assisting the architect with whatever skills he obtained from his Beaux-Arts training was an army of craftsmen. Craft skills abounded in the country at the turn of the century. Let it be said in praise of the Beaux-Arts architect, in sharp contrast to his Modernist successor, that he gave the craftsman the opportunity to exercise his skill to the fullest, a necessary, vital human reward today's architects deny the lesser toilers in the artistic vineyard. With good reason did the men (most of English origin) working on the William Kissam Vanderbilt mansion that stood at the northwest corner of Fifth Avenue and West 52 Street place a statue of Hunt, in the outfit of a stone carver, mallet and chisel in hand, on a pinnacle of the roof. The statue currently occupies a niche at the Harold Vanderbilt house, now a museum, at Harbor Hill, Long Island. (The plaster model is in the Museum of the City of New York.)

Not only did the architect have the craftsman on hand, he also had the skilled draftsman to do the thousand drawings a great building required. A good number of architects took pains to design every inch of their buildings, down to the humblest doorknob—nothing was left to chance. An office had to have a crew of men capable of executing the drawings and of making the endless changes that seemed to have been part of the ritual of creation. Interestingly enough, in the office of Carrère & Hastings, for a number of years a majority of men were graduates of the Ecole.

The key element that identifies what we call Beaux-Arts is not the rule of locking facade to plan, the emphasis on symmetry in the plan, or the eclecticism, but the powerful drive for embellishment. We can see it in New York's old bishop's-crook lamppost of cast iron, in the old fire-alarm posts with their Art Nouveau ornament, or the old iron-and-glass subway entrances. It can also be found in the monuments about the city, especially the war memorials (this being the generation before memorials had to be "useful"). Even Rockefeller Center, where, comparatively, ornament was more or less forgotten, had its sculptors and mural decorators. We think of Louis Sullivan as an apostle of the Modernistic, with his message "form follows function." In his own time he was known as an outstanding ornamentalist. His palette of decoration even extended to the human figure, as seen in his Bayard Building.

What draws us to these buildings and monuments, what commands our wonder, is embellishment. It is the key element in bringing visual delight to our great city.

1

1. Former United States Custom House, Bowling Green, 1899–1907, by Cass Gilbert. The federal presence has long manifested itself in lower Manhattan. There is Federal Hall Memorial (formerly the Passport Office, the Subtreasury and, originally, the Custom House) at Wall and Nassau Streets. No. 55 Wall Street, now the downtown headquarters of Citicorp, originated as the Merchants' Exchange and became the second Custom House (the successor to the one on Wall and Nassau). This, the third Custom House, in turn gave way to the present one in the World Trade Center.

That the Custom House should have had, in the old days, such importance was natural enough in a port city, but especially in the city which was and still is the nation's chief port. In the last century, when this great building was opened, customs was by far the chief source of federal revenue. The principal aspect of the Custom House in the last century was political, for, if City Hall was a Democratic fief, the Custom House was the Republican one. The building stands because Chester A. Arthur, before becoming Vice-President under James Garfield, was Collector of Customs of the Port of New York and, as such, stood high in the Grand Old Party. On becoming President in 1881, he took the initiative to see that the city obtained a proper custom house. A competition for the commission, held in 1899, was won by Cass Gilbert (1859–1934), a little-known architect from Minnesota who had only just completed the state capitol in St. Paul. Gilbert was something of a prodigy. His education was irregular but it was given its shape—for the talent was there—in the office of McKim, Mead & White, where Gilbert was assistant to Stanford White himself. After winning the competition for the Minnesota state capitol in St. Paul he went from triumph to triumph.

What Gilbert produced for the Custom House competition (as did the other competitors) was a building which, if it did not resemble any contemporary French building, did have some kinship with the designs produced by Frenchmen competing for the Grand Prix de Rome.

The facade attains its monumentality by having a giant Corinthian Order rising from a high rusticated base. The entablature, with its decorated frieze, carries a massive attic with a balustrade behind which is a mansard with elaborate copper flashing. The stone is granite, which contributes much to the monumental effect.

What brings the label "Beaux-Arts" to mind in such buildings is not so much the style, which is most often Classical, but the abundance of sculpture. The Custom House offers a prime example. So lavish a building could only have been produced when federal architecture, then under the aegis of the Secretary of the Treasury, was designed to reflect the power of the federal government. As a result, the sculptor had a key role in embellishment. The four groups at the base are the work of Daniel Chester French. Karl Bitter did the cartouche at the center of the attic, framed by two winged figures and topped by an eagle with spread wings. The freestanding figures on the attic are the work of Francis E. Elwell, Frederick Wellington Ruckstull, Augustus Lukeman, François Tonetti-Dozzi, Louis H. Saint Gaudens, Johannes Gelert, Albert Jaegers and Charles Grafly.

Nor is the sculptural detail less imposing. Much of it evokes the sea and commerce. Marine symbols are seen in the dolphins and tridents; commerce is represented by Mercury. In its abundance of ornament, the Custom House is one of the more rewarding buildings in the city. Ornamentation is carried into the interior by the large oval mural (*An Ocean Liner Entering New York Harbor*), executed in true fresco by Reginald Marsh.

2. Standard Oil Building, 26 Broadway at Bowling Green, 1922-26, by Carrère & Hastings with Shreve, Lamb & Blake. Credit for conceiving this great skyscraper is customarily given to Harold Pratt, an official of the old Standard Oil Company and a member of the family that founded Pratt Institute in Brooklyn. Certainly he chose wisely in turning to Thomas Hastings. (John Merven Carrère had died in 1911, but the firm's name remained unchanged.) The Standard Oil Trust, as it was first called, had settled at No. 26 on moving to New York from Cleveland in 1885. From here John D. Rockefeller ruled his empire. He would arrive daily from his house on West 54 Street (torn down to make way for the garden of the Museum of Modern Art). With the dissolution of the trust in the 1900s, the site became the headquarters of the Standard Oil Company of New Jersey, now known as Exxon; it was to remain here until moving to Rockefeller Center in the 1930s.

This view is north, as seen from the entrance to the former United States Custom House. It shows the narrow side of the tower facing Beaver Street; the curving front looks out on Broadway and the north end of Bowling Green.

The dramatic elements are the three-story-high Ionic columns and pilasters, first on the base structure, then above on the tower. Nowhere else in the world are found columns hundreds of feet in the air. They are part of the great skyscrapers, and they help to remind us

that America's greatest contribution to the Classical tradition is the Classical skyscraper, of which 26 Broadway is one of the finest.

Other Classical devices are also present: quoins, balustrades, shields in scroll frames and obelisks. But it is at the top of the tower that the architect's fancy achieved its reward. On a stepped pyramid stands a colossal bronze tripod (the world's biggest?). One of New York's great sights on a bright winter's day is to see plumes of steam escaping from it, for the tripod conceals a chimney or a vent. It is as if the denizens below were sacrificing to some ancient god, possibly to Mercury, the god of commerce.

Here, as elsewhere in lower Manhattan, the lobby is worth a glance. On the frieze of the marble hall are panels bearing the names of the original members of the Standard Oil Trust. To read them is to evoke a whole facet of American history: Rockefeller (John D. and William), Pratt, Flagler, Harkness, Bostwick and the other oil magnates. However brief the passage of the mighty corporation, it left a monument that ranks among the best of American office structures.

3. New York Stock Exchange, 8 Broad Street, 1900-03, by George Browne Post. The New York Stock Exchange is a very successful building. It was no mean feat on the part of the architect to make so low a structure, set among high buildings, command the street. Post

had acquired his Beaux-Arts training in the old atelier of Richard Morris Hunt back in the 1850s. His work, to say the least, is mixed. Much of it is long gone and need not be mourned. Here he triumphed (at the age of 63).

We are accustomed to a base for a colonnade, but it is customarily one, not two, stories high as here. The ground-floor openings are square-arched with round-arched windows above. Part of the monumental quality of the two-storied base, conveying a sense of power, are the massive volute brackets supporting the balconies.

There is nothing quite equal to columns of the mighty Corinthian Order, these being 52 feet high. It is easy, on seeing the Stock Exchange, to understand why the Corinthian was so popular in the Beaux-Arts era. There is much nonsense written about its being an imperial order—it was, it is true, a Roman favorite and is really more Roman than Greek, but the fact remains that it is a beautiful order, one which makes full use of the acanthus leaf and one of the best for achieving a sense of the monumental. Any political system is free to make use of it.

The pediment is big, as is the attic, with its cornice of lion masks. To see a pediment filled with sculpture is refreshing; too often in New York it is wholly absent. There lies the Greek touch: Ancient Greek architecture seems to have consisted largely of structures for holding sculpture.

The statues, after the work of J. Q. A. Ward and Paul W. Bartlett, are not original. The first figures, being of marble, crumbled in the city's atmosphere and were replaced by hollow lead figures given a coating to resemble stone. They are very crude and do not bear close examination.

The marble facade of the building is nothing but a screen. Behind the colonnade is a glass wall, the kind so popular today, lighting the great trading room, one of the city's sights. Although the hall has lost something of its aura, filled as it is with a variety of mechanical paraphernalia, it is still the setting of the spectacle of brokers trading.

4. Governors Island Ferry Terminal, South Ferry, 1906-07, by Walker & Morris. This terminal originally housed the ferry boats that went to South Brooklyn. It now serves the United States Coast Guard, quartered on Governors Island.

That the building is of steel did not prevent the architects from applying ornament. The various details, such as the brackets on the elliptical arches, are modified versions of Classical ornament as found in turn-of-the-century French architecture. Above the bays are offices (originally designed as a recreation area) and, over it, where another floor stands today, was a roof garden with pergolas.

The ancient ferry terminal is successful because, although it is built of a modern material, it has been given so much detail. Unlike contemporary structures where the utilitarian would appear to dictate flat, plain surfaces, here the utilitarian has been given relief, and light and shadow, along traditional lines.

6

5 & 6. American Surety Building, 100 Broadway at Pine Street, 1894–96, by Bruce Price. Bruce Price (1845–1903) was noted not only for his designs; he was also the father of Emily Price Post, the arbiter of manners. His position as a leading architect was attained by his work in the city and Tuxedo Park, the fashionable residential enclave in Orange County, N.Y., which he laid out and embellished for Pierre Lorillard.

The American Surety Building was executed according to the standard Classical formula for the tall building, with a "base," "shaft" and "capital," taking its nomenclature from the Classical column. The base is very effective, with its colonnade of eight monumental Ionic columns two stories high with a single story (the third) serving as attic. Above them rises the shaft of 11 stories, and the top seven stories are given horizontal accents with cornices of varying width. Above the topmost cornice is an effective two-story attic. The whole facade, executed in gray granite, is very effective.

One pleasing device is the use of the human figure. The figures in deep relief are the work of J. Massey Rhind, the sculptor who did one of the sets of bronze doors of nearby Trinity Church and the caryatids of the main entrance of Macy's on West 34 Street.

Here is another office building whose lobby should be visited. Although there have been changes over the years, it still boasts the black-and-gold ornament that makes it a rarity in the city. Overhead, the coffered ceiling is black, with abundant detail picked out in gold. On both sides below it are friezes.

5

7. Federal Reserve Bank of New York, Liberty, Nassau and William Streets and Maiden Lane, 1927–28, by York & Sawyer. As the most important bank of the Federal Reserve System, it is proper that this branch be housed in a massive structure worthy of Florence in its great days. Recognizing the adaptation of the Tuscan arch of the first-story windows, one knows the source. York & Sawyer, the firm that won the competition for its design, turned unabashedly to the great Italian city for inspiration.

This view shows the main facade on Liberty Street. Rustication is carried the full height of the building because the building sits on a single plot with four unequal sides. Although this treatment in no way resembles its model, Philip Sawyer, the designer of the firm (Atelier Redon at the Ecole), pointed to the rustication of Florence's Pitti Palace as his source. The medieval note of the building, for it is a mixture of the Gothic and the Classical, is seen in the machicolations at the tenth floor. They are repeated at the top of the building.

One peculiarity of the facade is the limestone from Indiana, which was selected to weather in different tones. At one end of the gray spectrum it is very light, as is customary, at the other, quite dark, which is unusual. Another distinguishing feature is the big wrought-iron lanterns at the entrance. Designed by Philip Sawyer, they were made by Samuel Yellin of Philadelphia.

The building is one of the city's more impressive, conveying at once the role of New York as the financial center of the nation. Underscoring this role is the fact that it is the Federal Reserve of New York which handles all financial transactions with the central banks of foreign nations. In its vaults are stored the gold bars for the accounts of these same banks.

The beholder will discover that much of the visual power of the edifice is due to the fact that, like its medieval progenitors, it is surrounded by narrow streets and high buildings. Were it in the open and approached by wide avenues, much of this impact would be lost.

8. Liberty Tower, 55 Liberty Street at Nassau Street, 1909, by Henry Ives Cobb. In the Progressive Era, very few Chicago architects, having achieved prominence, moved to New York. Henry Ives Cobb was one of the exceptions, and Liberty Tower is the most conspicuous of his New York buildings.

This view was taken from Chase Manhattan Plaza. Liberty Tower is in the center with the fortress of the Federal Reserve Bank of New York on the right.

Liberty Tower is a white terra-cotta Gothic skyscraper antedating the Woolworth Building (also in the Gothic and of terra-cotta) by four years. The lower stories have some detail, especially at the entrance, where there are niches with finials and crenellation. The shaft is spare; at the top enrichment takes over. Crouching figures with grotesque heads form the brackets beneath the first cornice. On the roof gables are finials (massive in size to be visible from the ground) and seated eagles and seated lions holding shields. The architecture buff may well ask himself why the Gothic did not become more popular. Its emphasis on high, bare shafts would appear to make it readily adaptable for the central part of the skyscraper, and the variety of decorative elements, modestly adopted here, would be fully exploited in the tower.

The poet William Cullen Bryant published the New York *Evening Post* on this site for several decades in the middle of the last century. Franklin Delano Roosevelt had his office in the present building in the 1920s, when he was vice-president and New York representative of a Baltimore bank. By that time, No. 55 was known as the Sinclair Building, the headquarters of Harry Sinclair, whose name hit the front pages as a result of the Teapot Dome scandals. In 1980 Liberty Tower was converted to cooperative apartments, one of the first examples of such a conversion in lower Manhattan.

9. Chamber of Commerce of the State of New York, 65 Liberty Street at Nassau Street, 1901–02, by James B. Baker. One of the challenges facing an architect designing a low building in the city is to give it a prominence in a setting dominated by towers. Baker faced such a hurdle when devising a headquarters for the Chamber of Commerce. The first story is made a massive platform by having a deep rustication and a batter. On it were placed half-engaged columns of Scamozzi Ionic with fluted shafts. Adding to the presence is the curved mansard above the attic. Its dormer windows are set in splendid frames whose broken round pediments have volutes with garlands.

The beholder may be puzzled by the blank walls between the columns. Originally they served as backdrop to three groups of

sculpture by Philip Martiny and Daniel Chester French. Unfortunately, they were of marble which eroded and had to be removed. The same fate met the figure of Mercury by Karl Bitter that once stood over the entrance. Structural note: 25,000 tons of white marble went into the revetment of the facade.

The special attraction of the building was the Great Hall or Chamber, its walls lined with portraits of the great American businessmen who built the nation, forming the finest collection of its kind. Regrettably, some of the collection has been sold.

10. Woolworth Building, 233 Broadway at Barclay Street, 1910–13, by Cass Gilbert. "The Cathedral of Commerce," opened in 1913 when President Wilson pressed a button in the White House to illuminate the building, became at once the symbol of a triumphant America. As the nation's tallest building, 792 feet high, it surpassed the Flatiron Building as an attraction, holding first place as the tallest building until the completion of the Chrysler Building in 1930. (The latter, in turn, was surpassed by the Empire State Building in 1931.)

Although Gilbert worked chiefly in the Classical style, he was, like the graduates of the Ecole des Beaux-Arts, an eclectic. In the instance of the Woolworth Building, he abandoned the Classical for the Flamboyant Gothic (French Gothic in its last phase) as the best style for an isolated tower.

This is the most successful example of the adaptation of the Gothic style to a skyscraper. By making use of the massive piers and shafts of the Gothic cathedral, Gilbert achieved a triumphant verticality. Gothic tracery also proved readily adaptable, as seen in the lower stories and the filigree of the tower.

Seven-foot-high polished granite forms the base, atop which is a two-story layer of Indiana limestone; the rest is terra-cotta, which permitted elaborate and varied ornamentation. As in the Gothic, it allowed the inclusion of many grotesques, such as gargoyles, and beasts, both mythical and real.

The explorer in the city should not overlook the lobby, where the combination of the marble floor and walls and the glass-mosaic vaulting, by Heinigke & Bowen, is quite startling. As if to balance the opulence, Gilbert introduced a less solemn note (keeping within the Gothic tradition). At the arches of the vaulting are stucco brackets tinted to resemble stone. What sets them apart is they take the form of caricatures of those associated with the building's construction, modeled by Donnelly & Ricci. We can see Frank Woolworth bent over, counting his nickels and dimes, and Gilbert, wearing a pince-nez, clutching a model of the tower.

11

11 & 12. Home Life Insurance Building, 255 Broadway between Murray and Warren Streets, 1893–94, by Napoleon Le Brun and Sons. At first glance the beholder puts this building down as a period piece, reacting to the abundance of detail set in a minor scale.

The three-story base might easily be divorced from the facade to serve a low structure. The ground floor is rusticated, with three arch bays framed by entrances with a Scamozzi Ionic. The three arched bays of the ground floor are repeated at the second story, only with more trappings in the form of engaged Corinthian columns, a broken entablature and lunettes above, set in the arches. The middle arch has figures in the spandrel. The fourth floor is chaste by comparison, with its small windows with arches and shallow rustication. Only at the center is a pair of windows given an elaborate frame with a round pediment resting on pairs of pilasters. The pilaster shaft, as is customary, is severe, but at the top ornament bursts into a second flourish. Order stands above Order, over the windows are swags with fluttering ribbons. The roofline has anthemia and short obelisks, while the copper-green roof rises with a diamond-shaped peak.

So narrow a building is very much part of the cityscape. The ornament is an attempt to convey the structure's importance. While we may deplore the visual chaos that is so much part of the New York street, we cannot help but accept this modest tower as part of the sharawaggi (studied lack of symmetry) endemic to the city skyline.

13 & 14. Former New York Times Building (*right*), **41 Park Row at Nassau Street, 1889, by George Browne Post. Former American Tract Society Building** (*left*), **150 Nassau Street, 1896, by R. H. Robertson.** A typical example of Beaux-Arts eclecticism is to be found in two Romanesque towers standing across from City Hall. The style had been initiated by Henry Hobson Richardson during the 1870s, notably in Boston's Trinity Church. New Yorkers have forgotten that it gained a major foothold in the city and continued to flourish for two decades, as seen here, fading around 1900.

The Romanesque is identified by the round arch and the massiveness conveyed by the revetment of rock-face ashlar. Modified machicolation at several of the stories links the building to the medieval style. Post also gave it a touch of the Gothic in the colonnettes.

The American Tract Society Building resembles the Times Building only in the use of rock-face ashlar in the lower stories and in the round arches. The Classical is present in the detail, the main attraction being the top floors, where the arches rest on Corinthian columns. At the corners on the Nassau Street side, the arcade is open and is adorned with winged figures, probably angels, because the American Tract Society was a publisher of religious literature. From its founding in 1825 to the first decade of this century, it printed millions of books and tracts in over 100 languages.

Both buildings are now owned by Pace University.

15. Municipal Building, Chambers and Centre Streets, 1907–16, by William Mitchell Kendall of McKim, Mead & White. No other American municipality houses its employees as splendidly as does the City of New York. The Municipal Building is without rival.

As with so many great works of the period across the country, the design was the result of a competition. Charles Follen McKim, nearing the end of his career, was against having the firm submit a design, for he did not like skyscrapers and frowned on the entrance of the firm into competitions, but the younger partners, headed by William Mitchell Kendall, won out.

The plan of the building was in part dictated by the site at the city's disposal, taking the form of a broad, shallow U with flattened sides. This view shows the inside of the U, facing Chambers Street. To gain more space, Kendall made the structure bestride what was a part of Chambers Street, which it does very effectively, the tunneled entrance being inspired by that of the Farnese Palace in Rome.

Once again we see the tripartite division of the Classical skyscraper: an elaborate base, a plain shaft and, at the top or capital, a series of temples shaped into a tower. The whole is of a beautiful gray granite.

The base is distinguished by a colonnade of monumental Corinthian columns across the mouth of the U with a high arch at the center, over the old extension of Chambers Street (now closed to traffic). Figures by the sculptor Adolph Alexander Weinman symbolizing Guidance, Progress, Civic Duty, etc. are in the spandrels and panels between the columns. Above the colonnade is an attic with the coats of arms of New Amsterdam and New York.

The Corinthian columns are repeated at the top of the building and in the temples of the tower. The use of columns high in the facade is seen on a number of city buildings, notably on the Helmsley Building at 230 Park Avenue.

At the very top is more sculpture, the statue of Civic Fame, also the work of Weinman. Twenty feet high, it stands on a ball, carrying a civic crown in its left hand and, on its right arm, a shield with the city's coat of arms.

The late John Barrington Bayley, designer of the new wing of the Frick Collection, and the leading authority on Classical architecture in this country, always maintained that the Municipal Building was the nation's finest skyscraper and the model for any attempts at executing a tall building in the Classical tradition.

13

14

10

16. Hall of Records, 31 Chambers Street at Centre Street, 1899–1911, by John R. Thomas and Horgan & Slattery. The city's finest Classical ensemble starts at City Hall and goes north to the New York County Courthouse. The chief link between the buildings, which vary in size, is the use of the Corinthian Order. First adopted at the Hall of Records, it was then used in the Municipal Building, in the County Courthouse and, last, in the United States Courthouse. The amateur of the Classical has, in these few buildings, a brief tour for studying several interpretations of the Order, which is even to be seen on the upper part of the facade of City Hall.

The main facade of the Hall of Records looks south onto Chambers Street and City Hall Park. Thomas set his columns on a high base of round arches. (On the building's sides, the columns give way to pilasters.) Above, a high entablature surrounds the building; behind it is an attic from which rises a pitched roof, almost a mansard.

A great virtue of the Classical is that it permits abundant sculpture; Thomas gave the sculptors and their partners, the stone carvers, a most generous welcome, to which they responded with ornaments including scroll frames in abundance and rostra on the corners of the fourth story.

Among the sculptors the architect invited was Philip Martiny, who did four groups at the street level, a pair being at the main entrance on Chambers Street and another at a now closed entrance on Centre Street. (The latter was moved to the porch of the New York County Courthouse when the street was widened.) On the attic, Martiny provided freestanding figures of local heroes, such as Peter Stuyvesant with his peg leg and De Witt Clinton of Erie Canal fame. Around the high central dormer rising from the attic is a cluster of figures by Henry Kirke Bush-Brown symbolizing the seasons, the arts and the ages of man.

The Hall of Records might be declared the epitome of Beaux-Arts because of its abundance of sculpture. At the time it was built it was considered very Parisian. In fact, the lobby and central hall, with its staircase of Siena marble, has a full Parisian flavor clearly inspired by Garnier's Opéra in Paris. And all of it came from the drawing board of a self-taught architect who had never seen Paris. The Beaux-Arts connection here is Philip Martiny, who was born in Strasbourg and had studied in Paris.

17. Manhattan Bridge Approach, The Bowery and Canal Street, 1904–09, by Carrère & Hastings. New York can boast of many of its bridges. One of them, certainly notable for its approaches, is the Manhattan Bridge. We must lament the loss of the Brooklyn approach; mindless highway improvement destroyed it when highway building raged unopposed. The only evidence that it once existed are two statues by Daniel Chester French which were saved by moving them to the entrance of the Brooklyn Museum, where they look somewhat lost. Even the Manhattan approach has been battered; gone are the balustrades that once framed the approach to the north and south.

But we can savor what is still there, a triumphal arch (one of the city's three) and the colonnades on either side consisting of Doric columns set on pedestals to convey greater sense of height. Above the entablature is a balustrade—so important in such structures because it creates an awareness of scale.

The arch, inspired by the Porte St. Denis in Paris, is splendid. It has a wide single opening framed by a rusticated band. Above is a large rectangular panel by Charles Cary Rumsey (the brother-in-law of Averell Harriman) depicting a buffalo hunt.

On the piers above the doorways at either side are pyramidal reliefs with heroic groups. The one on the north represents the Spirit of Commerce; that on the south, the Spirit of Industry. They were carved by Carl A. Hefer.

We can only wonder why such arch-colonnade ensembles were not adopted more often in the great decades of our architecture. The device is such a good one.

17

16

18. The Bowery Savings Bank, 130 The Bowery at Grand Street, ca. 1893–95, by McKim, Mead & White. It is a surprise to come on this monumental building, with its high Corinthian Order, on a thoroughfare so far past its glory days. When it was built, it must have been difficult to see, for The Bowery was literally filled by the posts and overhead tracks of the Second and Third Avenue elevated railroads!

The building is L-shaped; this is the facade of the wing looking out on Grand Street at the corner of Elizabeth Street. It was claimed, on the basis of the monumental portico and the lofty interior banking hall, that this was the first truly splendid bank building in the city. Certainly the Order is very impressive, as is the presence of sculpture (found less often than one would expect) in the pediment. In fact, one of the great weaknesses of the American Classical is the absence of sculpture in pediments, here corrected by the work of Frederick MacMonnies, best known for his groups on Brooklyn's Soldiers' and Sailors' Monument.

The pediment also has acroteria in the shape of anthemia, the main one being at the peak, with two secondary ones at the foot of each raking cornice. Behind the pediment is an attic with a row of lion masks and a row of antefixes. All three—acroteria, lion masks and antefixes—are very much part of Greek temple architecture.

The facade is nicely framed by Corinthian pilasters, reflecting the porch columns. Between pilaster and column, in addition to the window with a cornice rested on ancones and a rectangular sunken panel above with an elaborate frame, there are three coffers between the pilasters' capitals. The coffers are unusual in that they consist of a series of unadorned frames receding to a small square. They must be one of the firm's inventions.

As in the best of New York buildings, there is a reward in the interior. The banking hall, in a Corinthian Order with shafts of polished marble, has a ceiling with a high cover with hexagonal coffering. Not surprisingly, on its opening, the bank was hailed as setting a new standard for bank architecture, and it was imitated to the end of the Beaux-Arts era.

19. Roosevelt Building, 478–482 Broadway at Broome Street, 1874, by Richard Morris Hunt. The Roosevelt Building is a very modest survivor of the work of Hunt. In 1874 he could boast a substantial practice with the Stuyvesant Apartments (the city's first apartment house) and the Presbyterian Hospital to his credit, as well as the Marquand Chapel at Princeton and the Marshall Field house in Chicago. Soon after, he would be at work on one of the city's first skyscrapers, the Tribune Building on Nassau Street, a site now occupied by Pace College.

The Roosevelt Building is a small structure with a front of cast-iron, the building material which became so popular in the Civil War Era. Instead of the customary direct adaptations of the Classical,

Hunt's facade represented a more studied and more elaborate application. The ground floor has short pilasters in the style called Neo-Grec, in vogue in Paris in the 1850s. Above, we find columns and pilasters in the Scamozzi Ionic. The slender colonnettes within the three bays allowed the extensive use of glass. At the fourth floor are spandrels of open metalwork. All in all, it is more a curiosity than an historic building.

The distinctive name of the building stems from the fact that it was built by Roosevelt Hospital, now part of the St. Luke's–Roosevelt Hospital Center, from funds left by its founder, the lawyer James Henry Roosevelt, who had his office on the site.

20

21

20. Former Police Headquarters, 240 Centre Street at Broome and Grand Streets, 1909, by Hoppin & Koen. Although it suffered vandalism and a long delay before conversion to cooperative apartments, the old Police Headquarters building is still very much with us. It has survived simply because it is a fine building and no alternative use was proposed for the awkward site. The lot, formerly occupied by butcher stalls of the Centre Market, is shaped like an elongated flatiron, the narrow end at the north.

The structure's ground floor is rusticated, with round-arched windows, above which are Corinthian columns and pilasters rising two stories. Above the entablature is a balustrade with flaming urns on the posts—not a common sight in the city. Behind the balustrade is a two-story attic.

The entrance, with two statues, has been given particular emphasis with a four-column porch rising to a pediment. Seated on the pediment is the female figure of Manhattan with a turret crown. The four other boroughs are represented by four maidens, also mural-crowned. The tower consists of a column drum, a high dome, and a column lantern.

21. "Little" Singer Building, 561–563 Broadway at Prince Street, 1902–04, by Ernest Flagg. One of the distinguishing characteristics of the American graduates of the Ecole des Beaux-Arts was how little influenced they were by French architecture of the latter part of the nineteenth century or the first decades of the twentieth. An exception was Ernest Flagg (1857–1947). He was particularly taken by the exposed use of iron and of glass.

In this instance, a 12-story loft building, with facades on Broadway and Prince Street, ironwork is used decoratively with glass and terra-cotta. The result is a curiosity. The main influence came from Viollet-le-Duc, the restorer-theorist and father of Modern architecture who had called for the use of new materials, such as cast iron and glass, and for the "expression" of the function of supporting members in design.

Ernest Flagg was a graduate of the Ecole des Beaux-Arts, Atelier Blondel, who designed, among other projects, the United States Naval Academy in Annapolis. He was very proud to be a Paris man, even preserving his oval ID card from the school. While in Paris he kept a meticulous diary. With his papers and ID card, it is now in the archives of Avery Library at Columbia University.

Flagg was a founder of the Society of Beaux-Arts Architects in 1894 and its president from 1911 to 1913. The outstanding result of the activity of its members was the Beaux-Arts Institute of Design (today the National Institute for Architectural Education) which fostered architectural training, with ateliers across the country and competitions on the model of the Ecole.

22

23

22 & 23. Cable Building, 621 Broadway at Houston Street, 1892–94, by McKim, Mead & White. In the brief interlude between the horsecar and the electric trolley, the cable car provided transportation on a number of New York thoroughfares. Machinery to operate the cables, which ran just below street level, was housed in buildings along the route. The Cable Building contained the machinery for this stretch of Broadway and the offices of the Broadway Cable Traction and Seventh Avenue Railway Company.

The eight-story facade is divided by three superimposed arched bays, the first two stories high, the second four and the third two. The bays at each level are set off by simple pilasters; the first has beribboned fruit swags at the capital, the second necking with rosettes, and the third an enriched echinus and abacus. Above the topmost row, at the frieze, are elaborate scroll frames with cabochons. The topmost cornice has the customary lion masks and, over them, acroteria alternately large and small. Altogether a pleasing facade for what is essentially a modest building.

The main entrance is emphasized by its circular window framed by a bay-leaf wreath on which two torch-bearing maidens rest outstretched arms—one of those embellishments that give such enjoyment to the New Yorkers who are fond of exploring the older parts of the city.

24

24. Engine Company 33, 44 Great Jones Street off Lafayette Street, 1898, by Ernest Flagg and Walter B. Chambers. In recent years an unfortunate change has occurred in the construction of such civic structures as fire stations and police stations: They are now being incorporated in commercial buildings. Practical as this policy may be, it is a blow to the street setting and to civic pride. Of the two municipal departments, Fire almost always had the better architecture in its buildings at the turn of the century. This may well have been due to a stronger esprit de corps dating from the pre–Civil War generation of volunteer firemen. There was also the fascination of the equipment: the more and more elaborate fire trucks, and, of course, the superbly trained horses used before the coming of the internal-combustion engines.

It is rewarding to come across the old fire stations—especially this one, because one of the architects was Ernest Flagg who also designed the "Little" Singer Building. It tells something of the skill of Flagg and his colleague that they achieved the monumental in so small a structure. The rusticated base is a common device, but the wide arched bay placed on it was something of a novelty and makes the building grand. The sides and the arch of the bay have a curved chamfering. This betrays French allegiance, as it is often found in eighteenth-century French work. The elaborate scroll frame around a cabochon adds a nice touch to the bay's keystone. Originally it served as base for a flagpole that extended up through the cornice and the roof.

To underscore the monumental scale of the bay, the architects used a minor scale in the bay's windows. The framing, the bars, the cornice and the modified entablature inside the bay are of metal with small detail. The same minor scale is found in the wrought-iron railing at the base of the bay. It is quite evident that the facade has received excellent care over the years, or much of it would not be there today.

25 & 26. Bayard Building, 65–69 Bleecker Street between Broadway and Lafayette Street, 1897–98 by Louis Sullivan. The Chicago architect Louis Sullivan remains the hero of contemporary architects. Here is the apothegm, quoted in context, which has made him so respected among the Modernists: "Whether it be the sweeping eagle in his flight, or the open appleblossom, the toiling work-horse, the blithe swan, the branching oak, the winding stream at its base, the drifting clouds, over all the coursing sun, *form ever follows function,* and this is the law. Where function does not change, form does not change."

Sullivan may have declared it law, but he was not one to hold to it in his own designs. In his day he was best known as a skillful ornamentalist, not as a theorist of design. The Bayard Building offers an excellent sample of his decoration, even to having, beneath the deep overhang, rare winged figures. As are the figures, his ornament is realistic, with the thistle leaf omnipresent. He was able to achieve such fine detail (and so much of it) by using terra-cotta. Since the detail is repetitive, a few molds could be made from which the ornament could be cast. Sullivan's ornament was unique; only a few architects in the Midwest followed him in its use.

The first several floors are weak; Sullivan seems unresolved in linking the street level and the upper stories. To obtain the best view of the building, it is worth going south to study it through the narrow trough of Crosby Street. The vertical emphasis achieved by the thick unbroken shafts, with thin round shafts between, is the glory of the building.

New Yorkers curious about Sullivan's work see him at his best in the Bayard Building.

27. De Vinne Press Building, 399 Lafayette Street at East 4 Street, 1885, by Babb, Cook & Willard. Theodore Low De Vinne (1828–1914) was one of the great printers of the latter part of the nineteenth century. Anyone familiar with the publications of the period will recognize the names of *Scribner's Magazine*, *St. Nicholas* and *Century Magazine*. De Vinne also printed the *Century Dictionary*. The press was known for its fine-line wood engravings. In addition, De Vinne was a founder and president of the Grolier Club, the city's charmed oasis for bibliophiles, and the author of several books on printing.

This part of Lafayette Street (formerly Lafayette Place) was the center of the book trade, which had been drawn to the neighborhood by the Astor Library several hundred feet to the north. (The building is now occupied by the Public Theater.)

To house his presses and his bindery, De Vinne turned to the firm of Babb, Cook & Willard, remembered today for the Andrew Carnegie mansion (now the Cooper-Hewitt Museum), on Fifth

Avenue and East 91 Street. What they produced here was a massive red-brick structure in what might be termed Roman Utilitarian, a style best seen in the ruined buildings of Ostia Antica, the port of ancient Rome, and in what remains of the Roman aqueducts. Even the slight pitch of the roof is reminiscent of the Roman utilitarian structure.

The key element of the facade is the superimposition of rows of round-arched windows. Here there is no automatic pattern of small over large, nor are the windows limited to round arches, as seen in the presence of segmental arches. By balancing several window shapes, the architects obtained a monumental facade without ornament. The only accents are the vertical rows of quoins on the corners and at the entrance, and disks in the spandrels of the entrance arch. The absence of ornament in a structure of this era may come as a surprise, but we must remind ourselves that it is, after all, utilitarian.

For an actively used industrial building it has withstood time extremely well.

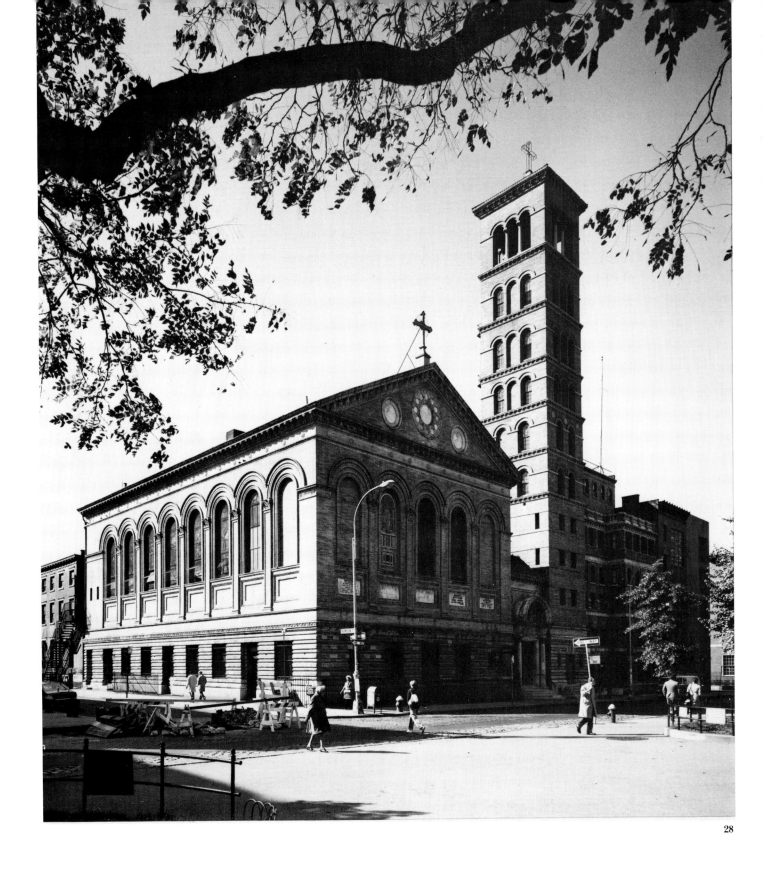

28. Judson Memorial Church, Washington Square and La Guardia Place, 1888–96, by McKim, Mead & White. In both its setting—Washington Square—and in its designer—the great firm of McKim, Mead & White—Judson Memorial Church is something of a curiosity, a structure of Roman brick in the North Italian Romanesque style in a neighborhood which, even today, is largely of red brick and white trim. The tower calls to mind many similarly inspired churches by Maginnis & Walsh in eastern Massachusetts. The actual model for the Judson, however, is San Miniato al Monte in Florence.

Stanford White is credited with the design, as he is for the porch of St. Bartholomew's on Park Avenue and East 51 Street, which follows that of St. Trophîme in Arles, a monument in the French Roman-esque. The eclecticism of White was typical of the age of Beaux-Arts.

Notable ornaments of the church include the stained-glass windows by John La Farge and a baptistry with a bas-relief executed by Herbert Adams after a design by Augustus Saint-Gaudens.

The church, chiefly funded by John D. Rockefeller, Sr. is named for the Reverend Dr. Adoniram Judson, a Baptist missionary who translated the Bible into Burmese and produced the first Burmese-English dictionary. The church has strong associations with literary Greenwich Village; Frank Norris, author of *The Octopus* and *The Pit*, once lived in the tower. Restored by the late Joseph J. Roberto, the structure is now owned by New York University and is called Judson Hall and Tower.

29. Washington Square Arch, Washington Square, 1889–92, by Stanford White. "The lamentable little Arch of Triumph which bestrides those beginnings of Washington Square," was Henry James's comment in 1905. One cannot help but feel that he felt a certain resentment against its presence on what had been his childhood playground. The square was very much part of his youth: His parents had been married in a house that once stood on the north side, and he himself was born only a block to the east of the square.

We, on the other hand, must be grateful for it. New York, after all, has a long road to go before it obtains its rightful share of monuments. At least it can boast of three triumphal arches: this one, the Manhattan approach to the Manhattan Bridge, and Brooklyn's Soldiers' and Sailors' Monument.

In 1889, a temporary arch of wood was built on Fifth Avenue, directly north of the site of the present one, as part of the centennial of George Washington's inauguration. New Yorkers were so elated with what they had wrought that they decided to erect a permanent arch in the square. Stanford White obtained the commission and it was completed in three years at a cost of $128,000.

Like all the great architects of his time, White was very familiar with ancient and recent examples. He noted that single-span arches were rare, citing the Arch of Galerius on the Via Egnatia in Salonika (Thessaloníki). A key difference in his Washington Arch was that it had no Orders. The measurements are: 86 feet high, span 30 feet 2 inches wide, piers 10 feet wide.

Basically, a triumphal arch is nothing more than a useful stand for sculpture, of which there is a sufficient amount here to make up for the absence of the Orders. The spandrel figures are the work of Frederick MacMonnies, a sculptor often associated with White, as at the Bowery Savings Bank. The eagle over the arch is by Philip Martiny. The two freestanding statues of Washington portray him as Commander-in-Chief (by Hermon A. McNeil) and as our first President (by A. Sterling Calder).

30. United Mutual Savings Bank (former Union Square Savings Bank), 20 Union Square at East 15 Street, 1907, by Henry Bacon. The palette of the Beaux-Arts ranged wide. This small bank, by the architect of the Lincoln Memorial and the designer of the standard lamppost for city parks, offers the Classical of the ancients in a severe form. Other than the Corinthian Order (a Roman Order), there is little ornament. The columns are very effective, standing on a low stylobate. The capitals, instead of bearing fleurons, carry eagles. The plain entablature is topped by a balustrade.

Why a balustrade? Obviously no one has access to the roof. It does, however, give scale. Balusters were unknown in ancient times. Like the scroll frame, they are an invention of the Renaissance, the first ones presumably being those in the Sistine Chapel.

In the upper-left corner of the photograph is an Ionic colonnade, part of the tower of the Consolidated Edison Building at the corner of Irving Place and East 14 Street.

31. Siegel-Cooper Building, 616–632 Sixth Avenue at West 18 Street, 1896, by DeLemos & Cordes. What is it that makes us go to Sixth Avenue to see these old department-store buildings? They are certainly not beautiful, yet somehow they draw us, much as some wooden mansions of the General Grant Era do. For one thing, we take a certain interest in any building that evokes the city's past. For another, we are bored with the barrenness of much of today's architecture. Actually, it is this boredom with (if not wholesale rejection of) today's architecture that has turned so many people to preservation. When Siegel-Cooper was built, no one talked of saving old buildings. Now there is a powerful movement, a sort of rearguard action against Modern architecture, whatever form it may take. So we have become fond of the Siegel-Cooper, despite the awkwardness of its facade.

The entrance, with three short barrel vaults, with coffers with rosettes, resting on broken pediments, is sufficiently grand. Above the center bay is an aedicule framing a window. We can list its parts: volute brackets, a balcony partially curved, a pair of Tuscan columns, two broken entablatures that support a round arch with an acroterion. And just inside the arch is an elaborate scroll frame. There are columns of Scamozzi Ionic, round windows with scrolls, wreaths and garlands and even panels beneath the cornice with lion masks from which hang husks. Even the cornice has its lion masks. We may have reservations about the facade's design, but it is a useful dictionary of ornament.

Siegel-Cooper was an unsuccessful attempt by a Chicago company to invade New York. For a decade or so it was an attraction, particularly for its fountain in a central atrium, which boasted a large statue, a smaller version of the *Republic* that Daniel Chester French had modeled for the World's Columbian Exposition of 1893 in Chicago.

32. Adams Dry Goods Store, 675–691 Sixth Avenue at West 22 Street, 1900, by DeLemos & Cordes. For a brief period Sixth Avenue around West 20 Street became a major shopping center. Several large department stores were built, the fronts of which astonish us in the Age of Boutiques.

There is something awkward in the design, as if the architect had not digested the elements at his disposal. The two-story base, with its arched bays, seems too high in relation to the three-story columns above. It appears almost higher than what it carries.

The poor proportions rob the design of the quality it should have, because the Scamozzi Ionic Order and the ornament are entirely suitable. The keystones of the bays are admirable, the center one bearing the head of Athena, the two to either side lion masks. The medallions bearing the initials ADG, nicely framed with wreaths, are suspended from fluttering ribbons. Nor can one fault the Ionic capitals except to note that they form a part of columns that are too short.

In the first decade of the century there would have been flagpoles rising from the attic with flags waving in the wind; below would be crowds of shoppers. One of the attractions in the vast store was a central court rising to a glassed-in roof. It must have been something of a relief from the avenue which, in those days, was covered by a noisy elevated railroad.

30

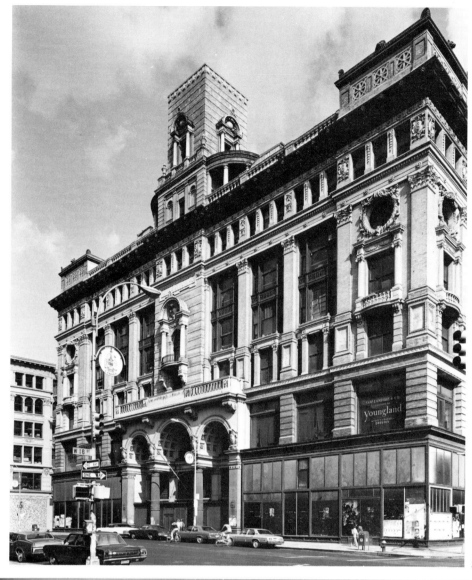

31

32

33. Judge Building, 110 Fifth Avenue at West 16 Street, 1888–89, by McKim, Mead and White (altered 1903). In addition to the old *Life*, for decades there existed in the city a second comic magazine, *Judge*. Having its offices here, it lent its name to the building, which housed a variety of publishing firms, including *Frank Leslie's Illustrated Weekly*. (A third, older magazine called *Puck*, which disappeared into the national chain of Hearst newspapers, had been superseded by *Life* and *Judge*.) In 1985 No. 110 returned to publishing when it was bought by *The New York Times* as offices for the company's magazine group.

The building was erected for Robert and Ogden Goelet, members of the New York family long involved in city real estate. In design it originally resembled Babb, Cook & Willard's De Vinne Press Building on Lafayette Street in that it was in the Roman Utilitarian Style. The ground floor on the street retains wide windows with segmental arches, those in the avenue being recently restored. The second and third floors were encompassed in equally wide round-arch bays; the arches both on street and avenue have been put back. At the fifth and sixth floors were high, narrow round-arch bays. The eighth floor had a row of small round-arch windows. As in the De Vinne Press Building, it resembled the tiered arched openings of an ancient Roman aqueduct, a resemblance carried even further by having, on the cornice, an attic wall pierced with arched openings. In 1903 the arches were removed, the bays were squared at the top, and three stories were added. The aqueduct touch remains in the two-story-high bays of the top addition.

The mixture in materials adopted is the familiar one of McKim, Mead & White—thin, long yellow Roman brick and terra-cotta trim.

34 & 35. Flatiron Building (originally the Fuller Building), at Broadway, Fifth Avenue and East 23 Street at Madison Square, 1901–03, by Daniel H. Burnham. Of all the skyscrapers built in the first decades of this century, the Flatiron Building was the one that captured the public imagination—even more than did the Woolworth Building (1913). The exigencies of the triangular site, its apex pointing up the avenue, dictated the plan, and the public at once baptized the structure the Flatiron Building. (The apex, it should be noted, is rounded off at a width of only six feet, which adds considerably to the startling effect when the building is viewed from the north.)

By the turn of the century, Fifth Avenue had long been established as the city's parade ground. For everyone, including the natives, a ride (it cost one thin dime) was obligatory on the double-decker horse-drawn omnibus (with the new century, on a bus with a French Berliet rotary engine). The Flatiron and its neighbor, the Metropolitan Life tower, had the horizon here pretty much to themselves.

Daniel H. Burnham was Chicago's leading architect. Here he did what he had done in his Chicago office buildings, executing a series of repetitions at each floor, giving the several facades a horizontal pattern. The ornament, spread evenly, is that of the Italian Renaissance. Only at the top, at the apex of the triangle, do we find some variation in columns with shafts made of drums of alternate widths—a device popular in the French Renaissance. So we have the mixture of several Classical styles common in the work called "Beaux-Arts."

Burnham was a force in his time. He was at the head of the architecture arm of the World's Columbian Expostion of 1893 and he produced the Chicago Plan of 1909. And it should not be forgotten that he headed the MacMillan Commission of 1901 which helped to make Washington our great Classical city.

In the foreground of No. 35 is Randolph Rogers' statue of William Seward, Abraham Lincoln's Secretary of State. It was Seward who secured the purchase of Alaska from Russia in 1867. For decades the territory was popularly known as "Seward's Folly."

36. Metropolitan Life Insurance Company Tower, Madison Square at East 24 Street, 1909, by Napoleon Le Brun & Sons. Metropolitan Life, a large life insurance company, has centered its operations on Madison Square for many years, beginning on the northwest corner of Park Avenue South and East 23 Street and expanding until it occupied two whole blocks north to East 25 Street. When the tower was completed, the company made it its symbol.

Rising 700 feet (51 stories), it was once one of the tallest buildings outside of lower Manhattan. When installed, its clock commanded attention, for its face is 26½ feet in diameter and its minute hand is 17 feet long. The tower is a greatly enlarged bell tower or campanile, modeled after those in Northern Italy, especially that of Venice. The tower is effective because it has a high arcade at the top, above which is a high sloping roof culminating in an elaborate lantern.

What we have today is not exactly the tower as built. In 1962, during a period when it was fashionable to strip buildings of ornament to give them a Modernistic look, the tower lost much of the detail that had added so much to the play of light and shade on the four facades. Gone are the rustication of the corners, the machicolation beneath the arcade. The arcade spandrels were denuded and a balcony with a balustrade removed. So, as effective as it still is, the tower must be judged with a note of caution.

Napoleon Le Brun (1821–1901), a Philadelphian, began his career in the office of Thomas Ustick Walter, an architect of the United States Capitol. Le Brun designed what is one of the finest Catholic churches in the country, the Cathedral of Saints Peter and Paul on Logan Circle in Philadelphia. The firm is identified with a number of firehouses in New York City, particularly the former Engine Company Number 31 Station on Lafayette and White Streets, a château of the Loire set down on a New York street. When this tower was built, Le Brun's sons were the senior principals in the firm.

37. Former Public Baths, Asser Levy Place and East 23 Street, 1904–06, by Arnold Brunner and William Martin Aiken. One of the great advantages of working in the Classical style is that it offers license to apply decoration in abundance. Certainly this is true of the Classical that comes under the head of Beaux-Arts, for painting and sculpture at the Ecole in its heyday were on a par with architecture. There was not the divorce in the arts, nor the outright dismissal of painting and sculpture by the architect, that are found today. Also, the humblest structure was considered to be as worthy of ornament as the noblest.

At one time, the city had a number of public baths; the one on Asser Levy Place survived because a swimming pool, built in the rear, continues to be used. It is a building that scores nicely on the Beaux-Arts checklist. It is divided into two wide-arched bays bordered by four pairs of Doric columns. The entablature is mutulary Doric. Metopes and triglyphs divide the frieze, and the cornice has deep mutules. The entablature, broken over the columns, carries paired vases with festoons of cloth. Behind them is a balustrade. To complete the design at the top is a cartouche with the city's coat of arms set in an elaborate scroll frame bordered by swags and cloth. The entrances are approached by a double flight of steps, and there is even a fountain between the two bays, consisting of a stalactite niche with a lion-mask spout.

Arnold Brunner (1857–1925) was, until recently, most famous for the original buildings of the Mount Sinai Medical Center. Since their demolition, he is best represented by the Federal Building in Cleveland.

38. Appellate Division, New York Supreme Court, Madison Square and East 25 Street, 1900, by James Brown Lord. This building might be said to represent the epitome of the academic tradition in the arts at the turn of the century. To help the architect, there assembled many of America's leading sculptors and painters (some of whose names are now forgotten) from Daniel Chester French to Edwin Howland Blashfield. Everything the courthouse stood for in the arts was the target of the famous Armory Show of 1913, held only two blocks to the east in the 69th (Fighting Irish) Regiment Armory.

The style is English Classical, resembling that of several large country houses with columned porches. The Order is Corinthian, the columns being set on tall bases to increase the sense of height. The first-story windows alternate round and ordinary pediments. In contrast, the second-floor windows were given frames with accented corners.

What commands notice at once is the abundance of sculpture, much as the Hall of Records and the Brooklyn Museum. At the entrance are seated heroic figures by Frederick Wellington Ruckstull (signed Ruckstuhl, the sculptor having used both spellings), in the pediment are figures by Charles Henry Niehaus. Above the pediment

36

is *Justice* by Daniel Chester French. On the attic of the street side stand *Zoroaster* by Edward Clark Potter, *Alfred the Great* by Jonathan Scott Hartley, *Lycurgus* by George Edwin Bissell, *Solon* by Herbert Adams, *St. Louis of France* by John Donoghue, *Manu* by Henry Augustus Lukeman and *Justinian* by Henry Kirke Bush-Brown.

One statue is missing—the figure of Mohammed by Charles Albert Lopez. Several decades ago, when the building was undergoing restoration, Muslim nations protested its presence as offensive to their religion, which is iconoclastic.

On the Madison Square side, the attic has four splendid caryatids by Thomas Shields Clarke, representing (left to right) winter, autumn, summer, spring. Above them, on the attic, is *Confucius* by Philip Martiny, *Peace* with two male figures by Karl Bitter, and *Moses* by William Cowper.

The interior has decoration to match, done by Kenyon Cox and Edwin Howland Blashfield (among others), under the aegis of John La Farge.

The cost of all this was as follows: the construction $422,468, the sculpture $157,000, the mural decoration $54,300—a total of $633,768. In no other building in the country has so much money, one third of the cost, been spent on painting and sculpture.

39. The Old Life Building, 19-21 West 31 Street, 1894, by Carrère & Hastings. This building housed the humor magazine *Life* (not the picture magazine of the same title published by Time, Inc.). The first *Life* was the vehicle for the wonderful drawings of Charles Dana Gibson, which pictured fashionable scenes. In its pages appeared the Gibson Girl, who helped form the female ideal of the turn of the century. Gibson was to become the owner of the magazine.

In the pediment over the entrance is a boy or cherub (the magazine's logo, placed at the head of each issue's table of contents), as well as the pair of L's in circles at the second floor, identifying the magazine.

As might be expected in a building from the drafting board of Carrère & Hastings, it has distinction. The first and second floors are given a special rustication. The broken pediment of the doorway is particularly fine. The windows, by the way, are French, not sash. Above the fifth floor is a cornice resting on large brackets of double volutes. The top three floors are inserted in an attic and a high mansard, a rare combination. The architects were ingenious in their handling of the insertion of three stories of windows.

Like all such facades, there is constant diversion as the beholder discovers elements which may have, at first, escaped attention, such as the quoining at the windows and the sides of the building. In the end, the eye descends to the doorway pediment to savor the beautifully carved figure of *Life*.

40. General Post Office, Eighth Avenue between West 31 and West 33 Streets, 1910-12, by McKim, Mead & White. The old Pennsylvania Railroad Station is gone, but the General Post Office, by the same great firm, remains. Having been built over railroad tracks, the building can present a facade with a width of more than two north-south blocks. In this way the partner in charge of the design, William Mitchell Kendall, could dispose a 377-foot-long Corinthian colonnade with a pavilion at either end. The columnar row is made impressive by the flight of steps, about 14 feet high. At the pavilions, instead of columns, there are Corinthian pilasters set on high bases. Becasue the colonnade is so splendid, we can forgive the architect for not having a visible entrance (to be found in the center of the wall behind the eleventh bay).

The colonnade upholds a modified entablature famous for the inscription on the frieze. A paraphrase of the description by Herodotus of the postal service of the Persian Empire, it reads: "Neither snow, nor rain, nor heat, nor gloom of night stays these couriers from the swift completion of their appointed rounds."

Above the entablature is an attic crowned by a parapet with antefixes, circles and volutes.

41. Macy's Department Store, Broadway and West 34 Street, 1901, by DeLemos & Cordes. Emile Zola, with his fascination for the innovations of his time, wrote a novel about department stores, *Au bonheur des dames* (1883). One can easily understand why, and only wonder why he was not imitated by a leading American novelist, such as Frank Norris. The big department store is an extraordinary institution, a giant bazaar or souk under one ownership and one roof. The very concept of gathering so wide a range of merchandise, displaying it, making it accessible to thousands and shipping it to the army of customers, remains one of the wonders of modern times and the store itself is a great spectacle.

There are visitors who, coming to a city, make a point of visiting the courthouse, the city hall, the main public park, the most popular churches and the department stores. They do all this long before visiting the art museum—and they are wise in doing so, for they see a city in action. And of all these places, the department store is the most fascinating.

New York's unrivaled department stores offer plenty of variety for the visitor, and not least among them is Macy's. Occupying a block roughly 200 feet by 700 feet, the store is vast. The view here is of the Broadway front. Compared with the two buildings to the south designed by the same architectural firm (the former Siegel-Cooper and Adams Dry Goods), the facade is subdued. The ground floor is obviously relatively new; originally it had some ornament as relief for the eye; the clock, for example is now in a box and not in an elaborate frame. Gone too is the roof's balustrade, with its columns and flagpoles—no doubt removed when a new floor was added. The rest is unchanged. The first three stories form a base, the second and third stories having horizontal rustication. The fourth to seventh stories are vertically joined by fluted pilasters of a modified Corinthian Order. The bays between the pilasters are filled with superimposed bay windows on three of the floors. Of greater interest are the sides of this portion of the facade, which are of brick. Inserted at the fourth-floor level are shallow aedicules consisting of engaged colonnettes and pediments. Inside the pediments are scrolls framing

cabochons. Higher up are vertically paired windows between which are lintels with swags carrying disks bearing the Macy star.

The attic above is two stories high with Palladian windows between vertical slabs. This device, common enough in American architecture since Colonial times, did not find wide use in the Beaux-Arts era. At Macy's it is a conspicuous feature, although it frequently escapes the notice of the amateur of architecture because it is at the top of the facade.

At the West 34 Street side, at the store's main entrance, are caryatids by J. Massey Rhind, who also did the figures on 100 Broadway.

40

41

42

32

43

Despite the change from Ionic to Doric and the loss of the window cornices, Altman's retains a grandeur that gives it a special niche on the avenue.

Samuel Breck Trowbridge was an *ancien* (graduate) of the Ecole des Beaux-Arts where he was in the Ateliers Daumet and Girault.

43. Former Tiffany Building, 409 Fifth Avenue at East 37 Street, 1903–06, by McKim, Mead & White.

Not many New York buildings have been inspired by buildings on Venice's Grand Canal. It would seem an excellent source for models: The watery thoroughfare of the Adriatic city was just as much commercial as residential because the Venetians, dwelling in the upper floors of their palaces, saved the lower floors for trading rooms and storage. Stanford White, who designed the building, took the superimposed Corinthian columns and the wide, arch windows of the bays from the Palazzo Grimani. He also adopted the third-floor balcony with its balustrade.

The result is a supremely successful building. It won praise from the fastidious Henry James, who saw it as a "great nobleness of white marble" (at the same time admitting that he rejoiced that it was not 25 stories high). But he could not help adding that it was "a more or less pious *pastiche* or reproduction." The comment is one of many revealing that James was unable to grasp the wonders of the American Classical in its ability to make use of European models, a failure shared by his friend Edith Wharton. In some ways, thanks to the proportions given it by White, the Tiffany Building is superior to the model.

The beholder is shocked by the vandalism inflicted on the lowest row of columns on the Fifth Avenue front. To obtain some idea of what they were once like, he must examine the East 37 Street side. With restoration now very much in fashion, it is a possibility that the old building will one day have its Corinthian capitals returned.

44. Former Gorham Company Building, 390 Fifth Avenue at West 36 Street, 1903–06, by McKim, Mead & White.

The Gorham Company, now part of the Textron conglomerate, is one of the nation's leading manufacturers of silverware. The old Providence, Rhode Island, concern had such a commanding position at the turn of the century that it had its own New York building. Gorham was also famous for its bronze work; it cast the pair of magnificent candelabra for the West 42 Street entrance to the New York Public Library, designed by Carrère & Hastings.

As often with McKim, Mead & White, the Italian palace served as inspiration. Here, the precise sources are not readily identifiable. Particularly nice is the Ionic arcade of the first two stories. The spandrels were originally filled with figures with outspread wings. The frieze above the arches has sculptured ornament. The top two floors are set off by a row of engaged Corinthian columns. We associate columns high in the air with the Classical skyscraper, such as the Helmsley Building at 230 Park Avenue, but the Classical architect freely adapted them to other building types, as we see here.

The most extraordinary device—one that is not found on any other New York building—is the deep cornice. To give it so large an extension, it has a double row of large modillions, all sheathed in green copper. Fifth Avenue boasts many splendid cornices, but, surely, this must be the most unusual.

The avenue front at the first two stories has been given today's "plastic improvement." One day, perhaps, it will be restored to its original appearance, much as the Corinthian capitals will be returned to the lower stories of the avenue front of the old Tiffany Building, a block to the north.

42. B. Altman & Co., Fifth Avenue and East 34 Street, 1906–14, by Trowbridge & Livingston.

Fifth Avenue remains the great bazaar of the nation—the Miracle Miles and Rodeo Drives of other cities and towns are as nothing compared to the segment of the great thoroughfare stretching from 34 to 59 Streets. Despite the erosion as merchandising has spread everywhere Fifth Avenue holds its own.

In the last century, New York's department stores had centered on Broadway, beginning far downtown on Chambers Street. By the end of the century, they were just below 23 Street and extended to Sixth Avenue. With this century came the great leap to the avenue north of 34 Street.

Altman's presents a severe Classical facade to the world. At the street level there are two-story-high Doric columns, four at the entrance portico having fluted shafts. The third story is marked by panels, followed by three plain stories. The two top stories are framed by two-story-high arched bays, splendid in their effect. A deep cornice crowns the whole. The total impression is one of sober elegance.

A little-known fact about the facade is that it was originally more elaborate (although entirely in keeping with the sober style). The columns had capitals of the Scamozzi Ionic. The windows of the now plain portion were set in frames with pediments, two floors of them with cornices resting on brackets. As there was not that much to strip away, one can only wonder why the owner went to the trouble. (Stripping architectural detail, although not quite as relentless as it once was, still goes on in the city.)

45. The Pierpont Morgan Library, 33 East 36 Street near Madison Avenue, 1902–07, by McKim, Mead & White. One of the more obvious landmarks in many an American city and town is the public library. It is particularly true of the small town, where the library building, customarily of stone or brick, stands out in a setting of clapboard houses. The Morgan Library, set on an open lot, bears a resemblance to one of those libraries, most of which are all stone and Classical.

But here the comparison ends, for the walls are of dry masonry—there is no mortar between the joints—and the facade is made not of thin marble revetment but of solid marble blocks. There is probably only one other building in the city boasting both features—the Federal Hall National Memorial on Wall Street. (The New York Public Library is sheathed in large blocks of marble with mortar.)

Charles Follen McKim was the architect. He gave the building a severe facade whose main feature is a central porch with a Palladian (or Serlian) bay. The columns, two pairs of columns in antis, are Ionic, while Tuscan pilasters divide the wings on either side of the porch. The arch of the center opening fits into an attic above, which is a modified entablature.

To mitigate the severity of facade, the sculptor Andrew O'Connor was called on to provide two panels, *Tragic Poetry* and *Lyric Poetry* (McKim's portrait appears in one of them) and other sculptural detail. The lions at the steps are the work of Edward Clark Potter, who also did the lions in front of the New York Public Library.

If the sculptors were invited to adorn the exterior, mural decorators were welcomed on the interior. H. Siddons Mowbray did the decoration of the entrance hall and the East Room, James Wall Finn that of the antique ceiling in the West Room.

A multitude of sources has been mentioned as the inspiration for the facade. The late John Barrington Bayley, designer of the new wing of the Frick Collection, pointed out in his *Letarouilly on Renaissance Rome* that the lower part of the Pietro Massimo Palace in Rome was an influence.

46. Consulate General of the Polish People's Republic, 233 Madison Avenue at East 37 Street, 1905, by Charles P. H. Gilbert. Few buildings in the city evoke "Beaux-Arts" as does the Polish Consulate General. There is plenty of detail and it is big, as seen in the brackets beneath the balconies and the cornices. The Beaux-Arts is underscored at the French window over the entrance. With a round arch, it has deeply curved chamfering and elaborate wood frames in the window itself. The high slate mansard, with copper flashing at the ridges, has plenty of ornament, including a silhouette of acroteria.

The amateur can list the Beaux-Arts refinements, such as the abundant rustication and the squat, flaming urns on the roof. It is comforting to think that it is now the property of a nation whose architectural tradition can boast equally florid buildings.

Nevertheless, the style somehow announces the parvenu. Indeed, it was built by one, the financier Captain Joseph Raphael DeLamar. Born in Amsterdam, he took to the sea, becoming a captain by his early twenties. He came to this country and went west to Leadville, Colorado. In 1878 he sold his mining interests and turned to Wall Street. DeLamar built the mansion for his wife, who promptly abandoned him, leaving him with his only daughter, Alice, and the house. Around 1940, Alice gained a certain prominence as patron of the arts and letters, mainly for funding the Surrealist magazine *View*.

47. Waterside Generating Station, Consolidated Edison Company of New York, First Avenue and East 41 Street, 1896-1900, by C. Wellesley Smith. There is a passage in Geoffrey Scott's magisterial *Architecture of Humanism* on the role of standards in architecture. Writing on the Classical tradition, he comments that, when the standards set by great men are high, even unknown architects can do pleasing work. A good example of this is the Waterside Generating Station. We know nothing of the building's architect, yet his design commands respect.

We can, of course, say that the facade mirrored too closely what lay behind it. Obviously, the machinery dictated the window at the left, as well as the fenestration at the right. But the response to function was part of Beaux-Arts instruction. Still, the architect did not let the engineer fix his part of the design. Instead of treating the building's envelope merely as part of a structure that might be called "a machine to shelter electrical machinery" (Le Corbusier: "A house is a machine for living"), C. Wellesley Smith gave form to the exterior. A particularly welcome device is the base of rusticated stone. Here the fenestration is square-headed and the segmental arches have diamond-pointed keystones. The main door, also square-headed with a keystone, even has a frame with crossettes. Above the doorway is a very tall window bay with a special handling in the form of a rusticated frame with curved chamfering and a large diamond-pointed keystone.

The several horizontal devices give unity to the whole. There is the water table, just above ground, a second projecting course, almost a modified cornice, above the rusticated stonework. Equally important is the modified entablature that serves as springing for all the arch windows, the large one and the four small ones. These horizontal devices are essential; binding the vertical devices, they create visual unity. There is no pretension in all this, simply the aim of the architect to achieve an attractive facade that otherwise could be forbidding.

A technological note: Waterside was the first power plant in the city to produce alternating current.

48. American Radiator Building, 40 West 40 Street at Bryant Park, 1924, by Raymond Hood. The Gothic had only a limited place in the Beaux-Arts spectrum. Much of it, even when not found in church structures, was archaeological in that the forms and details did faithful obeisance to the past, the Woolworth Building being the prime example. The rest of the structures, such as the American Radiator Building, offered modified versions of the style.

The bronze work of the ground floor has a touch of the Gothic in the vertical members around the entrance, the members also having plain finials. Beneath the third-floor balcony is a row of corbels, each of which carries a crouching figure, as found in the lobby of the Woolworth Building or on the misericords in the choir of St. Thomas' Church. For the most part, however, there is little enrichment, which gives the facade its general Modernistic appearance, although the tower reasserts the Gothic note in the form of open tracery.

The color scheme of the facade is striking. At the first story it is dark bronze against polished black granite. Black is carried into the lobby by means of marble and mirrors. Above, the very dark, almost black, brick is set off by gold terra-cotta trim.

Hood was one of the Gothic men who gradually turned Modernist. He came to public notice as a partner of John Mead Howells when, in 1922, the two won the competition for the Gothic Chicago Tribune Tower. He was subsequently the architect of the Daily News Building on East 42 Street and the former McGraw-Hill Building on West 42 Street.

49. Tudor City, East 40 to East 43 Streets, between First and Second Avenues, 1925-28, by Fred F. French Co. Tudor City is an apartment-house complex linked by its own north–south street, Tudor City Place. It stands to the west of the United Nations Secretariat, the glass rectangle seen on the right. To the left (north) is One United Nations Plaza.

The complex follows the standard pattern of the Classical apartment of the city, with its bottom floors (here five) having some ornament, then a bare shaft topped by floors with trim. In addition, at the top of the central building, shown here, are balustrades and high finials.

The east sides of these buildings offer blank walls to the world—something of a surprise. When Tudor City was built, the site of the United Nations was an industrial setting of railroad yards, carfloat slips, warehouses and slaughterhouses. The run-down properties were assembled by the late William Zeckendorf for purpose of developing the land, only to be sold to John D. Rockefeller, Jr., for use for the United Nations.

47

50. Bryant Park Studio Building, 80 West 40 Street at Sixth Avenue, 1901, by Lamb & Rich. Only a few years after his return from Paris, Richard Morris Hunt created a building that was very much a novelty in its day, the Studio Building on West 10 Street, designed to house artists' studios. That was in 1858. It was a novelty without imitations until the 1900s. One of the earliest in what amounted to a wave of studios was the Bryant Park Studio Building, built at the suggestion of an artist, Abraham Archibald Anderson. The imitations that followed were not necessarily built to house artists. Eventually the word "studio" was debased to mean simply a single-room apartment with enough space for a bathroom and cooking equipment.

The familiar Classical detail is present: rustication, keystones with volutes, pediments, balustrades resting on brackets. The acroteria that once graced the top cornice are gone. Rather than the detail, it is the large windows facing north (a necessity for the artist) that set the building apart. Certainly, facing Bryant Park, it was admirably designed for its tenants. In addition to the north light, the studios were spacious (Anderson's even had an organ with a battery of pipes). Artists are no longer to be found there.

51. Republic National Bank, former Knox Building, 452 Fifth Avenue at West 40 Street, 1902, by John H. Duncan. Gone are the days when the hat occupied an honored place on top of the head of the male New Yorker. Today, a gentleman no longer salutes a lady by raising his hat, for there is none to raise. One of the great names of New York hatdom was Knox, the hatter. His factory was in Danbury, Connecticut—the center of hat manufacturing—and his sales-and-office building was here.

To honor the avenue, much as his product honored the male head, Knox asked Duncan to design the building. Duncan, one of the outstanding men in the profession, had to his credit Grant's Tomb, Brooklyn's Soldiers' and Sailors' Monument and the City Council Chamber in City Hall. He was particularly fond of granite, of which he made good use here. The panels on the first-story blocks and the recessing of the blocks over the ground story underscore the stone's quality. A sense of power is conveyed by the monumental double volutes found beneath the cornice above the sixth floor. They must be among the largest in the city, as are the fruit swags found on those at either end of the avenue and street facades. The ornament begins to take on an imperial note as it goes up the facade. There are lion heads, three at the eighth floor (a monumental one at the top of the window in the central gable), shields with garlands at the ninth floor, and, on the rooftop, huge scroll frames and green copper trophies and torches fitted into antefixes.

For all the changes done to it in recent years, there is enough left to the old Knox Building inviting the passerby to pause and look.

52

52. Former Hotel Knickerbocker, 142 West 42 Street at Broadway, 1901–02, by Marvin & Vavis with Bruce Price. The Hotel Knickerbocker was built by Colonel John Jacob Astor, who also built the Hotel St. Regis. The building is the last of the hotels with mansard roofs that were once very much part of Times Square. Here Enrico Caruso stayed (the old Metropolitan Opera House was only two blocks to the south). Here once stood the King Cole Bar that was decorated by Maxfield Parrish's famous mural.

The fatal blow to many large New York hotels was Prohibition, which forced the closing of the bars and the restaurants. Instead of dining and drinking in hotels, people sought speakeasies which, if raided, could always migrate—a step denied a hotel restaurant. In 1920, Vincent Astor, who inherited the Astor properties (American

branch) when his father went down on the *Titanic,* called in the architect Charles Adams Platt to convert the buildings to offices. The Parrish mural went into storage, to be resurrected after Prohibition in the Hotel St. Regis.

The style here, French Classical, bears some resemblance to that of the old Life Building on West 31 Street in its brick and stone trim. The window treatment and the quoining in particular are alike, and both have a high mansard on an attic. The fenestration, with its triangular, round and broken pediments is a lesson in itself. The mansard has a special touch in its silhouette—the presence of high chimneys. The balustrade, with its urns, is the perfect topping to this Beaux-Arts cake.

53. Bowery Savings Bank, 110 East 42 Street between Park and Lexington Avenues, 1923, by York & Sawyer. The Ecole des Beaux-Arts was eclectic in its instruction, and so were its graduates, extending its influence even to Rockefeller Center. Of the two partners, Philip Sawyer was the Beaux-Arts man (Atelier Redon). While most of their work is Classical, they did break away to work in the Romanesque, as here, or in the Late Gothic, as at the Federal Reserve Bank of New York.

What characterizes their work, no matter the style, was the correct proportions, the handling of the enrichment of the ornament, and what might be called the finish. Nearly all their buildings have a distinct note of elegance. At the Bowery Savings, it is in the colonnettes on the splayed sides of the main entrance, the roll moldings (also known as bowtells) in the arch, where alternating colonnettes and moldings have been enriched with a cable pattern. It is also seen in the careful placement of square panels in the arch voussoirs.

The left part of the facade is almost Cistercian in its severity. Arcades are superimposed in three tiers, the openings getting smaller at each tier. The topmost, made of arches resting on colonnettes, is carried across the front well above the main entrance.

If the facade is of studied severity, the great banking hall behind the tall windows is not. There York & Sawyer unleashed their skill to decorate, still in a solemn way, with a variety of marble in quantity and some polychromy of painted ornament. The hall is Byzantine in its opulence, if not in style.

40

54. The New York Public Library, Fifth Avenue and West 42 Street, 1897–1911, by Carrère & Hastings. The New York Public Library (officially known as the Central Research Library of the New York Public Library) is one of the grandest buildings in the city. This is not surprising: The public libraries of American cities and towns are often the boast of the community. Certainly the New York Public Library takes its place easily among the finest such buildings in the country.

Among art historians, the building is considered the one that best exemplifies Beaux-Arts, although it is like no building ever built in France. At first viewing it is the enrichment of the main facade that invites the label Beaux-Arts. The steps and columns, the high central attic with its inscriptions, the wings that have, at the end, pediments filled with sculpture—these elements announce that this is a product of the greatest era of American architecture. The main influence is eighteenth-century French, particularly the work of Ange-Jacques Gabriel, architect of the Place de la Concorde in Paris (1755). But the sources of inspiration were not confined to Gabriel or the eighteenth century. The Celeste Bartos Forum (Room 80), with its glass ceiling, is influenced directly by the reading room of the Bibliothèque Nationale (1856–75), designed by Henri Labrouste.

Both Henry Merven Carrère and Thomas Hastings went to the Ecole des Beaux-Arts, the latter in the Atelier André and the former in the Ateliers Robert, Laisne and Ginain. Returning from Paris, they went to work for McKim, Mead & White, an incubator for the profession. After several years they founded their partnership and were already on the rise when they won the competition for the library in 1897. Probably no other building of the era received such attention from its designers. Anyone examining the facade and wandering through the interior soon becomes aware of the library's quality down to the smallest detail. The average citizen thinks first of the famous lions by the sculptor Edward Clark Potter, but they are only the most conspicuous of the embellishments. The bronze doors, the wood paneling of some of the rooms, the stucco ceiling of the main reading room—all proclaim the care and skill lavished with such splendid results by the architects, draftsmen and the multitude of craftsmen.

Other than the opulent Classical, here executed in white Vermont marble, it is the plan that reflects Beaux-Arts training. The balanced and symmetrical disposition of the rooms, the location of the stairs, the placing of the halls for proper circulation, the location of the stacks combine to produce an architectural wonder. And, as a final Beaux-Arts note, the facade we see before us reflects the balance and symmetry of the beautifully organized plan. Carrère & Hastings produced one of the nation's most splendid buildings.

55. Grand Central Terminal, Park Avenue and East 42 Street, 1903–13, by Reed & Stem and Warren & Wetmore. Of all the surviving great railroad stations, Grand Central Terminal is the most splendid by far, more so even than Washington's Union Station. The terminal was part of the extraordinary development of Park Avenue. Few other examples of civic improvement in the nation have equaled it, including the Michigan Avenue crossing of the Chicago River in Chicago (a modest effort by comparison) or the shaping of the Mall in Washington in the 1900s.

The terminal building is the keystone to the whole development. The great facade has high, arched bays separated by columns in pairs. The treatment is not uncommon; we know it from the New York Public Library, the Metropolitan Museum of Art and the American Museum of Natural History. Here the columns are French Doric; in the other three, they are Corinthian. Paired at the center, the columns are found singly at both ends along with pilasters, and the whole is framed by two high wide walls. Across the whole facade, above column and wall, is an entablature with a deep cornice.

The attic is particularly well handled. One of the weaknesses of the attic as adopted by American architects is that it is too bare, as in the Lincoln Memorial. In consequence, it is visually crushing, overly dominating. It is too important a part of a facade to be left unadorned. At each end Whitney Warren, the designer, placed round pediments with broken cornices in which he housed the seals of the state (left) and the city (right) with frames made of garlands. And he had much the same enrichment at the center, where the round part of the pediment is broken to make room for a giant clock, the ornament of which is in deep relief, so very effective in underscoring light and

shadow. Triumphing over the whole facade is the sculptural group made up of Mercury (the god of transportation), Hercules (associated with physical strength, and Athena (intellectual strength), while behind Mercury is a spread-winged eagle. The scale of French sculptor Jules-Alexis Coutan's work can be grasped when we learn that the figure of Mercury is 16 feet high and his outstretched arm nine feet long. Monumental sculpture of this quality, even in the Beaux-Arts era, was rare.

Everything about the facade deserves careful study—the bronze lampposts with their paired lanterns, the balusters of the balustrades, the Doric capitals of the columns, the ornament on the attic.

A bronze statue of the frock-coated Commodore Vanderbilt stands in front of the center bay. It was his grandson, William Kissam Vanderbilt, who headed the New York Central and saw to it that Whitney Warren became architect here. He also gave the final approval to Coutan's group. The Vanderbilts were the great builders in the city in the last century; Grand Central Terminal is one of their enduring monuments.

56. The Century Association, 7 West 43 Street, 1889–91, by McKim, Mead & White. Clubs were very much part of the post–Civil War years, although they were often housed in modest buildings. After 1880, with the Beaux-Arts era, came the grand buildings that were part of the city's seemingly endless expansion (interrupted by the occasional financial panic). One of the clubs, the ''intellectuals' club,'' was the Century Association. An institution that had begun as the Sketch Club, it had (and retains) the distinction of being a center for the arts and letters. Its building, erected when the association had

56

57

outgrown its building off Union Square, was to be among the first of a dozen or so to be designed by the great firm of McKim, Mead & White.

The facade is of long, thin yellow Roman brick and terra-cotta. The quantity of terra-cotta is surprising; customarily, it is limited to trim, but here it sheathes the first story and makes up the entablature and the top balustrade with its ornament. The rustication of the high first story serves as a base for the Corinthian pilasters of the second.

The style and materials allowed full freedom in selecting the decoration. Over the entrance there is a fine keystone with a lion mask. The first-story frieze is unusual in its chain band with rosettes; the main frieze consists of bound imbricated bayleaves and bayberries. The wrought iron, which appears Italian-Spanish, reveals the hand of White.

Leland M. Roth, the authority on McKim, Mead & White, credits White with the facade, McKim with the plan, and White's assistant, Joseph Morrill Wells, with the details.

The Palladian window over the entrance was originally part of an open porch. On the sidewalk, a foot or so in front of the building, were ten granite bollards. They disappeared when the sidewalk was narrowed.

57. Harvard Club of New York, 27 West 44 Street, 1893–94, 1902, 1915, by McKim, Mead & White. Club architecture would appear to have been almost the monopoly of two firms—McKim, Mead & White and Delano & Aldrich. The former, coming on the scene first, obtained the lion's share, certainly in the matter of large structures. The Harvard Club not only occupies a wide front on West 44 Street but also extends north on a large lot on West 45 Street.

Red brick, a material associated with the university, being called "Harvard brick," dominates on both fronts. Too often today brick is used alone; here it is relieved by limestone trim, particularly at the entrance and above the entrance in three-quarter engaged Ionic columns. The stone is carried upward in the university's seal and a cornice, topped, at the center, by a globe. The tall French windows, originally sash, on the second floor are a nice, urbane touch.

The interior may safely be described as "club style," that is, rooms paneled with stained oak and filled with upholstered leather chairs. The great room, known as Harvard Hall, is in the rear extension. Paneled in dark wood and three stories in height, it must have one of the highest ceilings in the city outside of a theater, a church or a library.

Originally, the entrance had a shallow porch of two Doric columns which disappeared when the sidewalk was narrowed.

58. New York Yacht Club, 37 West 44 Street, 1898, by Warren & Wetmore. The New York Yacht Club is in a class by itself. One can only wish that there were more buildings like it, because a great city has to have ornament in abundance, just as it has to have monuments such as equestrian statues, freestanding heroic figures and sculptured fountains. The great tragedy of our time is that we have been denied them.

At least we can console ourselves by walking west on West 44 Street from Fifth Avenue to view the Yacht Club. There is unalloyed pleasure in looking at this facade. There is no need to take courses in art appreciation to enjoy the stony spectacle; anyone can delight in it.

The monumental effect is achieved, as customary, by having an Order placed on a massive base. The Order is the Scamozzi Ionic, French division (marked by the husks hanging from the capitals). Above is a fine entablature with a deep cornice and a rare (at least on city exteriors) pulvinated frieze. The attic overhead is severe, but a balustrade takes over, with posts bearing square shafts with chamfered corners. Behind the balustrade is a terrace and a second attic with a mansard roof and dormers.

Some of the elements seem odd—square shafts on the posts and, on the right at the first attic, a pair of brackets with volutes that seem to serve no purpose. Originally, they were bases for two flagpoles that were fitted in the cornice above—the two holes are visible—and they rise alongside two massive shafts with niches. Space for the poles can also be seen in the cuts in rails of the posts. The other posts to the west (left) were part of a wood pergola that extended from the second attic.

All of this seems secondary when we look at the galleon sterns that adorn the lower part of the three main bays of the facade. They are wonderful, even in their having dripping stalactites extending over the top course of the base. The doorway to the right has its special ornament, a cartouche in an elaborate frame. And, above the doorway, is the mask of Neptune or some other sea god. Higher up, to either side of the mask, are clusters of marine trophies. What a building!

The nation's best-known yacht club is properly housed. The galleon windows front the high-ceilinged Model Room, where the walls are lined with the models of famous sailing yachts. It is in this room that the America Cup was kept until the Australians won it in 1983.

59. Yale Club, 50 Vanderbilt Avenue at East 44 Street, 1915, by James Gamble Rogers. Alumni associations are a conspicuous aspect of American higher education. They are the chief source of funds for private universities and colleges, and they are important allies in obtaining public as well as private moneys for public institutions. Quite naturally, it has followed that the more enthusiastic alumni have their clubs and club buildings. In New York, Yale alumni obtained a beautiful building by Rogers, the architect who came to design many of the buildings at Yale, and even Butler Library for Columbia University.

James Gamble Rogers may not have been an outstanding architect. In a sense, his talents were improved by the presence of more skillful colleagues. Certainly this club building is among his best work. The great New York architects of the day had already produced tall buildings in the Classical tradition; Rogers was simply following in the trail of his talented peers, for which he deserves praise.

The base of the facade here is high, comprising a low ground floor and a high second floor. It provides a perfect plinth for high Tuscan pilasters, which rise three floors. The fenestration of the second floor, with its round arches, fits beautifully in the rustication. And a nice touch is the scroll frame around the cabochon.

The architect made the proper use of rustication by having it frame the windows at the first two floors and by also having it at either end of the facade, where it continues all the way to the top of the building.

In a sense, the first six floors are a base for a high building. This particular base has been divided much as the facade of which it is a part, that is, into three distinct divisions. The third division, at the sixth floor, has an entablature with a high frieze, and it is the frieze where the architect put the sixth-floor windows. Nor did he forget to have some lion heads on the cornice.

58

59

61

60 & 61. Helmsley Building (former New York Central Building), 230 Park Avenue between East 45 and East 46 Street, 1929, by Warren & Wetmore. Despite the presence of Modern glass-skin structures, Park Avenue remains the great Classical avenue of the century. It was made possible by electric traction: Where this tower now stands was an open railroad yard, and the smell of this part of the city was that of smoke from locomotives burning soft coal. When electricity replaced steam, as mandated by the State, the yard was covered and the space was developed as a wonderful line of luxury buildings. Douglas Elliman, a leading real-estate man, was responsible for the change. From East 45 Street north to East 96 Street, the new thoroughfare became a double row of Classical apartment houses. Serving as center or keystone was 230 Park Avenue, built as the headquarters of the New York Central Railroad. Its designer was Whitney Warren, architect of Grand Central Terminal.

The tower ranks with those of the old Standard Oil Building at 26 Broadway, the Bankers Trust on Wall and Nassau Streets and the Municipal Building. Is there anything more dramatic than these three-story-high columns hundreds of feet above the ground, resting on giant voluted brackets? This breathtaking treatment adds a dimension to the Classical found nowhere else in the country.

Above the colonnade, the tower continues to volutes, balustrades and a pyramid roof whose peak boasts an elaborate lantern. The roof's dormers have intricate frames, particularly effective at the round and oval windows. The lantern, with its Corinthian columns and arches, its flaming urns and its pinnacle with volutes, is a princely aedicule in itself. Even the chimney stacks have been given a special shape of Venetian inspiration.

The architectural buff should not neglect the lower stories decorated with bison heads and, at street level, the bronze masks. The lobby is stunning with its trim of pink Languedoc marble contrasted with panels of polished travertine and handsome wrought-iron lanterns. The elevator doors and the elevator cabs may well be the finest in the city.

American railroads no longer dominate the community as they once did, but what grand monuments they gave our cities!

60

45

62. Charles Scribner's Sons Building, 597 Fifth Avenue near East 48 Street, 1913, by Ernest Flagg. The Paris men—the architects who went to the Ecole des Beaux-Arts—kept contemporary French architecture at arm's length, one of the few exceptions being Ernest Flagg. The influence is much in evidence at the "Little" Singer Building and a bit of it can be seen here. The storefront, with its cast-iron columns, doorway and window framing, is a clue, as is the use of the segmental arch in the seventh-floor windows. More evidence is in the handling of the cast iron inside the three vertical bays, three stories high.

In all this identification one has to be careful, certainly in a city where, for a generation, cast-iron fronts ruled in commercial architecture. There was plenty of cast iron in use in Europe at the time; in fact, it took a variety of shapes unknown here. Even Viollet-le-Duc, high priest of the functional and the use of the latest materials, made cast iron very much part of his work, always in a highly personal way.

The most effective part of the facade is the storefront, the wide windows permitting a good display of books and a view of the shelves of books within. For all the talk of culture in the great city, it is too seldom that books, at least, have had so prominent a place on the avenue as here.

The rest of the facade is marked by the steep, eye-catching mansard. At its base are two obelisks (a rare ornament in the city; only in lower Manhattan, at 26 Broadway, have they been given the prominence they deserve). In addition, there is a splendid central dormer two stories high. Here the windows are framed by a pair of figures in relief, herms set in sheaths. They uphold an entablature and pediment that boasts, at its peak, an acroterion. The stylistic mixture is Renaissance and Greek, typical of the work of some of the Paris men. The stroller should cross the avenue to get a better view of the mansard and its ornament.

63. RCA Building, 30 Rockefeller Center. Rockefeller Center, 1931–40, by Corbett, Harrison & Macmurray; Hood & Fouilhoux; Reinhard & Hofmeister. Although at first it would seem that Rockefeller Center could hardly be categorized as Beaux-Arts, there

are three arguments for doing so. First, the more active architects in the three firms involved were products of the Ecole: Harvey Wiley Corbett was there from 1896 to 1900 in the Atelier Pascal and Wallace K. Harrison in 1919 in the Atelier Umbdenstock. It is too often forgotten that the Ecole did not stand aside from fashion. Where it once was itself a source of architectural fashion, by the 1920s it was succumbing to what came to be recognized as Modern. Even before the building of the Center, such men as Corbett and Harrison were working in Art Deco, a form of Modernism which still had some ornamentation, although shallow and flat.

Second, arts other than architecture were given prominence because of the emphasis on decoration. If ornament in the older sense had vanished at Rockefeller Center, painting and sculpture remained. Not given the settings they once enjoyed, they are nevertheless prominent, the statue of Prometheus by Paul Manship, the murals in the RCA Building by José María Sert and other examples being notable. And the third Beaux-Arts element is the formal, balanced plan with low buildings carefully set against tall ones.

Central to the formal plan is the RCA Building. Here we have a high shaft—not quite a slab—of Indiana limestone given a chat-sawed surface, with emphasis on the vertical. The stone slab part of the design almost identifies the Center, as it is seen in its other buildings.

Another conspicuous aspect of the center that has nothing to do with the Beaux-Arts is the flat roofs. There are no towers, a feature common to tall buildings of the 1920s. Their absence is due to the prejudice of the chief engineer-developer in charge, John R. Todd of Brown & Todd, who disliked towers from a childhood prejudice and also dismissed them as useless commercially—no rentable space. Thus the towerless slab became part of New York architecture.

Even today Rockefeller Center enjoys a special distinction due to the Beaux-Arts influence in its plan and balanced elevations, on which score it has no rival. There is no winter spectacle to match the skaters in the sunken court placed next to the shaft of the RCA Building.

64. Former Villard Houses (the Helmsley Palace Hotel), Madison Avenue between East 50 and East 51 Street, 1882–85, by McKim, Mead & White. The Villard Houses might appear to be a single large mansion around a central court with two additional houses on East 51 Street. Actually, there were four houses on the court, two of which, those to the north and south, retain portions of their original interiors, while the two central houses serve as the entrance to the Helmsley Palace Hotel.

The complex is the oldest surviving work by McKim, Mead & White in the city. Previously, the partners, influenced by the Boston architect Henry Hobson Richardson, worked, for the most part, in the Romanesque. The Villard Houses represented their first step in the Classical, which was to distinguish their work.

Charles Follen McKim (who had attended the Ecole, Atelier Daumet, from 1867 to 1870) obtained the commission for the firm; the design came from Stanford White and his assistant Joseph Morrill Wells. Its most startling aspect is the placement of its four residences around the court. Another is that, being of one design, it looks like one house. Its source of inspiration was the Cancelleria, the great Papal chancellery building in Rome. The Villard Houses' shallow rustication, quoining and window frames all stem from the Roman building. With such a novel construction for the city, it is surprising that White turned to brownstone instead of to Indiana limestone, then being brought to the city by Richard Morris Hunt. (The Cancelleria is Roman brick and travertine.) It was the last important residence in the city to be built of this sandstone, which came from the Connecticut Valley.

The Villard Houses are a prime example of today's adaptive preservation. After being owned by various individuals and families over the years, the residences were gradually converted to offices, all of which eventually became the property of the Archdiocese of New York. When plans were announced to have the site cleared for a new hotel, a campaign to save them was initiated by the Municipal Art Society along with several other civic organizations. Working with real-estate magnate Harry Helmsley, the officers of the society found a solution by having the developer lease the property from the Archdiocese and having the hotel built behind the east front. The best rooms of the complex, in the south wing, were turned into the hotel's reception rooms. The north wing became the Urban Center, serving as headquarters for civic organizations including the Municipal Art Society, the Park Association, the Architectural League and the New York Chapter of the American Institute of Architects. It also contains the Urban Center Books, a bookstore specializing in books on architecture, landscape architecture, city planning and related subjects.

65. Cartier, Inc. (*left*), Fifth Avenue at East 52 Street, 1905, by Robert W. Gibson; 1917, remodeled by William Welles Bosworth. Olympic Airways Building (*right*), 647 Fifth Avenue, 1905, by Hunt & Hunt.
Cartier's was originally a residence built by Morton F. Plant, the traction magnate from New London, Connecticut, who developed the Florida West Coast Railroad. Myth has it that he sold the house to the well-known jeweler for some cash and a string of pearls. What actually took place was far less romantic. William Kissam Vanderbilt, whose famous mansion designed by Richard Morris Hunt stood diagonally across the avenue on the northwest corner of West 52 Street, had originally sold the site to Plant on condition that it be kept residential for a quarter of a century. With commerce migrating rapidly up the avenue, Plant sold the building for $1 million to Vanderbilt, who leased it to Cartier's. The jeweler then called on Welles Bosworth (Ecole des Beaux-Arts, Atelier Redon) to convert it for commercial purposes. (Bosworth is best known for the former

AT&T Building at 195 Broadway and the campus of the Massachusetts Institute of Technology.)

The large pediment on the East 52 Street side indicates where the main entrance of the residence was; when the building became a store, the entrance was shifted to Fifth Avenue. The facade has a rusticated ground floor with square-headed windows installed by Bosworth; the former entrance kept its round arch.

There are some very nice touches on the two facades. The second-story windows have engaged Ionic columns and full entablatures; those of the third, lintels on brackets and cornices on ancones. For fanciers of rinceaux, there are splendid examples in the frieze. The balustrade at the top has double balusters instead of the single ones seen in the neighboring building.

Of all the details, it is the fluted Ionic pilasters that are the most interesting. The capitals are Scamozzi Ionic, with the volutes treated with acanthus and with paired pendants of husks. The pediment

itself has an attraction, with its cornucopias to either side of the round window at the center. Altogether, it is a fine survivor of the grand era.

The Olympic Airways Building is the survivor of a pair known as the Marble Twins. In an attempt to keep this part of the avenue a residential enclave, George Washington Vanderbilt, the youngest son of William Henry Vanderbilt and the builder of Biltmore in Asheville, North Carolina, commissioned the Hunt brothers, sons of Richard Morris Hunt, to design the pair with a common front. (Young Vanderbilt lived at the time in one of his father's houses on the west side of the avenue.)

It was not long before the houses were converted to commercial use. In the transformation, the street floor was made to resemble that of Cartier's. On the fourth floor, which had been the top floor, rectangular windows replaced square windows, but the big rosettes were retained. An additional story was added and a modified cornice replaced the earlier one. The balustrade comes from the original building. Then No. 647 lost its twin to the south.

The chief distinction is the monumental Corinthian pilasters with fluted shafts, just one of several examples of the Order to be found on the avenue, the most familiar being that of the New York Public Library.

66. Racquet and Tennis Club, 370 Park Avenue at East 52 Street, 1917–18, by McKim, Mead & White. The Racquet and Tennis Club is one of the standouts of the Classical left in the part of Park Avenue that has become a Glassville. After seeing the repeated shiny surfaces, it is refreshing for the observer to stop here.

The architecture amateur is safe in calling the facade Tuscan, not only because of the use of the Tuscan arch but because of the generally sober treatment. The Tuscan arch was the trademark of York & Sawyer, seldom adopted by other firms. This club building, by McKim, Mead & White, is one of the exceptions.

The arch, set in the deep limestone rustication of the ground floor, commands attention. (As a base for a facade, arch and rustication are hard to surpass.) Above, the arch is found again in three central bays, rising two stories and forming an open porch. At the fourth floor, the arch is repeated, but the bays are blind. The brick, by the way, is that McKim, Mead & White favorite, the long, thin yellow Roman brick.

Two additional touches help shape the facade: the scroll frame over the center of the three open bays and the very deep cornice, a striking instrument to cap a facade, of which there are a good number in the city. Nor should the balustrade above the cornice be missed; we cannot imagine the building without it, which is, in a way, a good test of suitability.

67. River House, 435 East 52 Street, 1931, Bottomley, Wagner & White. River House is one of the most luxurious apartment buildings in the city. For all its simplicity, as seen in this view taken from Roosevelt Island, it has a flourish.

This panache can be found in the curious shafts rising from the fourteenth floor of the wings and the top floors of the tower. Today they could even be termed "Post-Modern." Rather it is the lanterns of the tower and the aedicule that conceals the water tank that convey the period flavor. Would Art Deco actually be the term for the decoration of the tower?

William Lawrence Bottomley, a Virginia architect, is best remembered for his substantial Colonial Georgian houses in Richmond.

River House was built in the Depression for the pleasure of six very wealthy men, one of whom was the late Marshall Field III, the Maecenas from Chicago who founded the Chicago *Sun* and funded the newspaper *PM*. The building also houses the River Club.

River House occupies a small niche in the history of the American theater. Its north flank was part of the set for Sidney Kingsley's play *Dead End*, a tale of juxtaposed wealth and poverty. At one point, a group of youngsters, the "Dead End Kids," climbed, dripping, out of the orchestra pit (representing the East River), the play having been written before the construction of the F.D.R. Drive. (Until it was constructed, River House residents had docking facilities for their yachts.) The Dead End Kids went on to success in Hollywood; today they are to be seen in the late-night movies on television.

68. Former Aeolian Building, 689 Fifth Avenue at East 54 Street, 1926, by Warren & Wetmore. Like York & Sawyer, Delano & Aldrich and McKim, Mead & White, Warren & Wetmore was one of those firms that had the instinct for civic embellishment even though the work at hand might be a private rather than a public commission. The beholder is free to make comparisons, severe perhaps, with his favorite buildings on Fifth Avenue, but he must concede that there is a place for the old Aeolian Building in the avenue's panoply.

The detail stems from the eighteenth-century French style, somewhat fragile for so large a building. It can be seen in the second-story windows with the double-curve heads hung with swags and in the reliefs of the flaming urns at the third floor. The facade has its plain spaces, the windows of the "shaft" having shallow lintels and no cornices. And the vertical panels between the windows are bare. Yet the bare effect is minimized as the eye catches the silhouettes at the top, where there are giant flaming urns, more garlands at the windows, balustrades and a fanciful aedicule with a bronze lantern concealing the water tank.

Since the building was constructed for a piano company, one searches for a musical description of it: a modest piece for the harpsichord with just a few flourishes—the double curves of the window heads, the swags, the urns and the "temple" at the top, which might have been lifted from an old garden.

The "improvement" on the ground floor is deplorable. There was no need to substitute unornamented polished travertine for ornamented limestone.

69. University Club, 1 West 54 Street on Fifth Avenue, 1897–1900, by McKim, Mead & White. More often than not, Stanford White is given the credit for the great firm's New York buildings. In the instance of the University Club, the palm goes to Charles Follen McKim. The art historian has a hard time identifying McKim's source of inspiration. Several Italian palaces can be cited, but it is obvious that the architect bowed to no particular one. This is refreshing; too often, in the academic game of pointing to sources, little initiative is left to the architect.

It is unusual to find a building with a wholly rusticated facade, here executed in Milford granite (the stone also found on the well-known terrace of the New York Public Library). In the facade McKim placed superimposed high round-arched windows, a fenestration of splendid sobriety. There is a mezzanine (or entresol) above the first story and one above the second, but they hardly intrude on the fenestration. Their square windows and carved panels bearing the seals of our great universities and colleges, modeled by Daniel Chester French, form a counterpoint, a relief to the all-pervasive rustication. Another counterpoint is provided by the masks in deep relief on the window keystones, the work of Charles

Niehaus, best known for one of the sets of bronze doors at Trinity Church. Keystones are one of the great devices of the Classical; New York, at one time, had many, but most disappeared with the fashion for the Modern. They seem easy enough to design, but there exist enough monstrosities to prove otherwise. What counts here is the deep relief and their placement on volutes.

Even the balcony railings make their contribution to the facade: The bronze rinceaux with green patina are in themselves a strong visual element complementing the granite rustication.

The entrance is slightly forbidding—as it should be for a palace. On either side are engaged columns with shafts of alternating widths. Above the entrance, over the central window of the second story, is a big cartouche bearing the club seal, designed by Kenyon Cox and modeled by George Brewster.

The presence of painter and sculptor is refreshing—too often architects have ignored their brother artists. If they have invited their contribution, it has usually been to give them hopeless places for embellishment. Here we have a model of how architect, painter and sculptor can work together.

70. Hotel Maxime's de Paris (former Gotham Hotel), 2 West 55 Street on Fifth Avenue, 1902–05, by Hiss & Weekes. Is it part of modern times that fashions of all kinds are of extremely short duration? Something—anything—comes into vogue and, after a few brief years, is gone. Take the hotel. It is an American invention, started ca. the 1830s, but the grand luxury hotel had its origins in the 1890s. It lasted about two generations, although some linger on. (I do not consider the large glass boxes as grand because Modern architecture, having no ornament, cannot convey the luxury identified with the luxury hotel.) The railroad was the impetus for the luxury hotel (just as the car and the airplane have been the impetus of the motel) for in the old days, one paused in one's travels.

At least the grand hotel has survived in part where the later movie palace has vanished from the American cityscape, to be resuscitated as a concert hall or a church.

Maxime's stands to the west of the St. Regis, a sliver of which can be seen on the left of the photograph. In fact, the two form a rare gateway, two pylons on Fifth Avenue. Both share similar decorative elements: rustication and devices such as the massive brackets beneath balconies and cornice. Maxime's, however, has windows with square arches, those at the corner being given a different touch with voussoirs in relief. The mighty cornice has high copper cresting.

The entrance is also outstanding for its female figures in deep relief.

The Gotham played a role in American history. It was here, in 1911, that Woodrow Wilson first met Colonel Edward House, Democratic boss of Texas. Both men realized at once that their destinies were joined and that Wilson would become President of the United States in the following year's election. House exercised considerable influence during Wilson's administration.

71. The St. Regis Hotel, Fifth Avenue and East 55 Street, 1901–04, by Trowbridge & Livingston. The high mansard, such as the one atop the St. Regis, is often considered peculiarly Beaux-Arts. Actually, New Yorkers had seen them long before 1900, the first one supposedly having been on a house on lower Fifth Avenue built in the early 1850s—an echo of the French Second Empire (which had great influence on American culture, from architecture to military uniforms). The hotel's mansard and the giant brackets beneath the balconies, the wrought iron of the balconies and the splendid pediments above the oval windows in the mansard might be called quintessential Beaux-Arts.

The St. Regis belongs to the opulent tradition of the mansard-roofed hotels found from the Mediterranean to the North Sea.

Railroad hotels come to mind, as do the large hotels built in spas and seaside resorts in different parts of the world.

The lobby is like the facade. A sign of its quality is that the hotel's successive owners have preserved the lobby. When changes have been made, such as the mural work behind the clerks' desk and on the ceiling, by the late Eloi Bordelon, they have been consistent in style. Off the lobby is the King Cole Room, where one of America's famous murals is lodged—*King Cole,* by Maxfield Parrish. The great illustrator—his work for books and calendars is still treasured—painted it for the former Knickerbocker Hotel on the southeast corner of Broadway and West 42 Street. It went "underground" in Prohibition to surface here after Repeal thanks to the thoughtfulness of Vincent Astor.

Who was Saint Regis? Saint Jean-François Regis, a French Jesuit who was a missionary to the French Huguenots, was canonized in 1737.

72. Carnegie Hall, West 57 Street and Seventh Avenue, 1891, by William B. Tuthill with William Morris Hunt and Dankmar Adler. For one of the world's great concert halls, Carnegie looks out on the world modestly. The style is Classical, almost Roman Utilitarian—it has the superimposition of arched openings that is best seen in the great ancient aqueducts. At the entrance are five high doorways with arches, although these last are made separate elements by a modified entablature that extends the length of both the street and avenue facades. Above the five doorways are five high bays with round arches and, last, a series of round-arched windows set in square bays. Even the high attic has a row of windows with arches. On the avenue side, high and low bays are blind—filled with masonry.

The tower, rising on the eastern flank of the street side, has tall square-arched windows, contrasting its angular lines as against the curves of the main building. The brick is brownish-yellow Roman; the sculptural trim is executed in terra-cotta.

The sober exterior is but a reflection of a sober interior. Listening to great music, even at the turn of the century, was a serious entertainment. In addition to making a pleasing structure, the designers triumphed by building a hall with wonderful acoustics.

Before leaving the hall, we might give two salutes, first to Andrew Carnegie, whose fortune made the building possible, and a second, possibly a whole battery of them, to the violinist Isaac Stern, who saved the building from demolition in the 1960s.

73. Art Students League (former American Fine Arts Society Building), 215 West 57 Street, 1890–92, by Henry Janeway Hardenbergh with John C. Jacobsen and Walter C. Hunting. This Renaissance building houses one of America's best-known art schools, the Art Students League of New York. Aspirants in painting and sculpture come from all over the country in their quest for training and success. The building was built by the American Fine Arts Society, which had been formed by the Society of American Artists (a group of French-trained realist painters and sculptors in rebellion against the National Academy of Design), the Architectural League, and the Art Students League. They all had their offices here, as did, at various times, the New York Chapter of the American Institute of Architects, the National Sculpture Society and the National Academy of Design. In this building were held the important exhibitions at the turn of the century, and the annual shows of the National Academy and the Architectural League. Their equivalents simply do not exist today.

To bring three art organizations together to share a building would be difficult at any time, even in those days, when architects, painters and sculptors still spoke to one another. What made it possible was the gift of George Washington Vanderbilt, the man who built Biltmore in Asheville, North Carolina. He also made possible the competition for its design won by Henry Janeway Hardenbergh, the architect of the Plaza Hotel and the Dakota.

The style, popular in the 1890s, is that of North European Renaissance, as revealed by the somewhat provincial ornament. The Classical tradition took many paths in those days. The North European was not uncommon. To either side of the entrance is a variation of the ancient Roman candelabrum in relief. (A good example of such candelabra exists in the New York Public Library.) The candelabra are repeated in the center of the second story, although, in this instance, instead of having finials, they rise to modified Corinthian capitals that must have been Hardenbergh's

invention. The capitals are found on the pilasters to either side of the facade, which have shafts with panels of arabesque relief. The pilasters are repeated on the third story. Similar relief is found above the small second- and third-floor windows. A nice touch is found on the attic where a parapet has posts with panels of cherubs in relief! We may wonder how many passersby—or art students, for that matter—know that there are small boys up there. (Pierce Rice, in his *Man As Hero: The Human Figure in Western Art,* points to the cherub as the symbol or identifying element of Western Art.) Above each post, providing a silhouette, are flaming urns with swags of cloth.

74. Queensboro Bridge, East 59 Street at First and Second Avenues, 1893–1909, by Gustav Lindenthal, engineer, and Palmer & Hornbostel, architects. The view is from the small park at the foot of East 57 Street and Sutton Place, by far the best place to see the bridge. For the anchorage and towers, the explorer is advised to go north on Sutton Place to East 59 Street, where there is another spectacular view.

What makes the Queensboro and the other bridges of the city so interesting is the architectural presence in the handling of the anchorage and the decoration of the steel members, notably the towers. The silhouette is very pleasing, especially at night, when the top parts are lit. In the daytime, the finials and rostra give the silhouette its special accent. Until 1960 flagpoles rose from the finials; then, in a fit of economy, the municipality cut them down. Certainly they should be brought back to restore the silhouette as one of the city's sights.

Design honors go to Henry Hornbostel, the architect who worked on the Hellgate Bridge to the north. He later moved to Pittsburgh where, among other structures, he designed the splendid City-County Building.

75. Con Edison (former Interborough Rapid Transit [IRT] Company) Power Station, West 59 Street and Eleventh Avenue, 1901–04, by McKim, Mead & White. We may well wonder why the great architectural firms, offspring of the Ecole des Beaux-Arts, were not given more commissions for large industrial and commercial projects. They were eminently suited to design them. In fact, the large structures presented a fresh challenge: How could the art of architecture best shape the new building types, such as a power-house? Perhaps the important firms had enough work without seeking commissions for buildings that did not require an architect, as did a large house or a college campus or a church. And there may have been an element of snobbery in passing over the industrial or plainly commercial projects. Fortunately, the city has one splendid example of industrial work by a leading firm, the old IRT power station, built to furnish power for the city's first subway line.

As might be expected, the basic planning of the structure was left to the engineers, but when it came to the exterior they bowed to Stanford White. He divided the facade into bays with pilasters, single on the avenue side (shown here), double on the street side. The pilasters are made of alternating recessive courses of brick and blocks of terra-cotta decorated with fronds. Above the pilasters is a modified cornice topped by an attic with a cornice (the latter long since removed). Between the pilasters are high round-arched windows, above which wreaths of terra-cotta in relief link keystones and a modified entablature. The brick is the buff Roman kind that the firm often adopted, the terra-cotta matching it in color. The four courses of the base are of Milford granite.

76. Metropolitan Club, 1 East 60 Street on Fifth Avenue, 1891–94, by McKim, Mead & White. New York, at least in its great era of architecture, believed in housing its clubs splendidly. Among the more luxurious club buildings is that of the Metropolitan. A newcomer among such institutions, it was founded by a group of distinguished members of the Union Club, among whom were J. Pierpont Morgan, Cornelius Vanderbilt (grandson of the Commodore) and Robert Goelet. Their choice of architect inevitably fell on the firm of McKim, Mead & White, with "Stanny" White the partner in charge.

The Italian palace facade was adopted here, as in the University Club. The first story is marked by shallow rustication and a cornice with a large balcony. Second-story windows have cornices, as do those at the third story, the latter with cornices resting on brackets. A fine entablature with a wide cornice tops the building. A specifically Roman touch is found in the details of the entablature, inspired by the Farnese Palace, the frieze bearing the lily of the Farnese.

This view shows the East 60 Street side, with its courtyard screened by a Doric colonnade. The wrought-iron gates, made by John Williams of New York, are typical of the quality of the crafts at the turn of the century. They bespeak a generation of craftsmen who were so much part of the Beaux-Arts era. Without the army of skilled artisans, the architects of the time would never have been able to achieve the wonders they did.

It was in these clubs that some of the great corporations were launched. Now such transactions have their beginning on the golf course—or is it at the airport?

77. Pierre Hotel, 2 East 61 Street, 1928, by Schultze & Weaver. A little-known firm, Schultze & Weaver did nicely in obtaining commissions for hotels. In addition to the Pierre, they could point to the Sherry-Netherland and the Waldorf-Astoria. The three demonstrate the firm's ease in handling several styles. As with so many architects, by the late 1920s the firm had a tendency to eschew ornament. Here, while the ornament is present, it is given shallow relief.

Although the hotel rises at the center, the facade, by having one-story-high wings, makes this part of the building appear much like a pavilion. It is a pleasing alternative to the usual treatment and a special courtesy to the beholder. At the center, on a base, are three high arched windows that light a large dining room. Framing them are pairs of Doric pilasters set on plinths. At either end of the pavilion are square-headed windows, also with pilasters, to mark the ends of the facade as well as to make space below for two doorways. On the roof of the wings are balustrades with large urns on the balustrade posts.

What is it about ornament that conveys the note of delight? The urns, the rhythm of the balusters, the shallow triglyphs with their guttae on the modified frieze, the keystones—all attract the eye and invite us into the pavilion.

And it is well worth stepping into this part of the Pierre. Off the corridor is a high-ceilinged foyer that leads to several dining rooms (one of which is behind the three center windows) and ballrooms. It is remarkable in its mural decoration in the Venetian manner, the work of the late Edward Melcarth, a New York painter who died in Venice. The murals depict youths and maidens in contemporary clothes wandering through gardens or going up and down terraces; overhead is a sky. Carved masks by the artist are set over doors. Even the marbling (stucco painted to resemble marble) was executed by Melcarth and his assistants. Done in 1958, it is the most recent of such decorations (among the most lavish in the city, the work of José María Sert having disappeared from the Waldorf-Astoria), but, being in a traditional style, it goes unnoticed.

76

77

78. Wildenstein Gallery, 19 East 64 Street, 1932, by Horace Trumbauer, with Julian Abele. Horace Trumbauer (1868–1938) was one of the great architects of the second generation of the Beaux-Arts era. Born in Philadelphia in modest circumstances, he was initiated into architecture in the firm of G. D. and W. D. Hewitt, a successful Philadelphia firm best known for the Bellevue-Stratford Hotel. (They were, respectively, the grandfather and great-uncle of the late John Barrington Bayley, designer of the new wing of the Frick Collection.) On his own by the 1890s, Trumbauer obtained, from the start, a wealthy clientele in Philadelphia and New York. He turned, wholly unself-consciously, to the French eighteenth-century style, which he skillfully adapted to the American setting. As a result of his unerring sense of proportion and scale, he often improved on his French models.

The Wildenstein Gallery, one of his last works, is a prime example of his skill. At the street level, four vertical panels separate three bays filled with a doorway and two high windows. What makes the arched opening so successful is the presence of sculpture, the masked keystones with sprays of laurel. At the second floor, the three bays are divided by four Ionic pilasters rising two stories. At the top is an entablature with a deep cornice resting on modillions. It carries a balustrade behind which is an attic with a slate mansard.

As at the ground floor, touches of sculpture give the facade interest. There are the brackets of the second-story cornices from which hang acanthus-leaf husks. Beneath the third-floor lintels are swags strung from fluted triglyphs. The volutes of the Ionic capitals carry swags. Even on the attic the parapet wall has a foliated Vitruvian scroll.

Adding to the general quality is the stone, a French limestone from the famous quarry of Saint-Maximin north of Paris.

But stone, sculpture, a Classical Order and tall windows would be as nothing without Trumbauer's masterly command of proportion. The student of architecture could do worse than study the dimensions of the various parts of this facade; what he discovers here is applicable to any style.

In designing the Wildenstein Gallery, Trumbauer was assisted by Julian Abele, a very rare instance of a black architect in a leading firm of the era. Abele had unusual talent which Trumbauer discovered when his assistant was quite young. He paid Abele's tuition in college and at architectural school, and even sent him to Paris.

When the histories of our architecture are rewritten, as they inevitably will be in another generation, Horace Trumbauer and Julian Abele will be among those, now neglected, who will be singled out as giants in their time.

79. Lotos Club, former William J. Schiefflin residence, 5 East 66 Street, 1898–1900, by Richard Howland Hunt. The eldest son of Richard Morris Hunt, Richard Howland Hunt carried on the work on the central wing of the Metropolitan Museum of Art after his father's death and, with his brother, Joseph Howland Hunt, continued his father's practice into the 1920s.

A glance at the slate mansard with its round windows (bull's-eye, or *œil-de-bœuf* in French) would indicate French influence—something of nineteenth-century Paris. Yet it has been carefully adapted for the New York setting, the ornament being far less abundant than, let us say, on the Ansonia on the Upper West Side.

The rusticated base (all horizontal grooves, none vertical) is standard treatment for the ground floor. The brick of the second and third stories is unusual for a house of this style, although it can be found in the old Life building by Carrère & Hastings, but its use is limited compared to the limestone with its carving. Certain touches are very pleasing. The round-arch bays of the second floor have curved chamfering inspired by eighteenth-century French work. Inserted in the arches are square-headed windows that allowed the architect to have fine scroll frames beneath the arches. Bolder ornament, but not too much, is seen at the dormers. Altogether, the facade is very satisfactory.

Today the seat of the Lotos Club, an institution noted for its cuisine, the building was once the residence of William J. Schiefflin. He came of an old New York family whose fortunes sprang from importing medical drugs and medicaments. In recent decades the family company became known as the importer of wines and liqueurs.

80

80. 131–135 East 66 Street at Lexington Avenue, 1905–07, by Charles Adams Platt. One of the great apartment buildings in the city and probably the finest work to come off the drawing board of Charles Adams Platt, this is called a studio building, although it never served an artist. What "studio" signified was an apartment consisting of one two-story-high room, the "studio," bordered by a duplex with bedrooms, baths and kitchen. The tenants experienced the reward of the arrangement when they moved back and forth between the one big room with a high ceiling and the rooms with low ceilings set on two floors.

For these apartments, the architect devised a beautiful sheath of Indiana limestone. The facade was broken into five parts rather than the customary three, each having its particular treatment yet combining into a successful whole. The first three floors have a familiar rusticated wall, the base for the rest. A wide, deep course separates the third and fourth floors, the fourth floor having a cornice to set it apart. The next stratification of two stories has its cornice. Platt placed the fifth- and sixth-floor windows in two-story-high frames with square arches and keystones, a brilliant solution to

breaking up the facade vertically. Not all the superimposed pairs of windows have frames; those at each end of the two facades, avenue and street, are simply set in the wall. The architect also broke the cornice where it runs over the frames, strengthening the vertical emphasis. The next four floors are plain, separated from the top floor by yet another cornice.

This stunning apartment house has a splendid entrance. To either side of the doorway are Roman Ionic columns upholding broken entablatures on which rests the pediment, broken in the middle. And there is a massive keystone set at the center of the frieze and architrave.

Another triumphant note is the topmost cornice. To appreciate its beauty, the beholder should stand as close to the building as possible. Almost directly above is the cornice soffit with modillions separated by coffers filled with rosettes. They built well in the Beaux-Arts era.

Charles Adams Platt had a career different from his architectural colleagues. He began as an etcher, being apprenticed to the father of the famous Maxfield Parrish. He then turned to painting, next to landscape architecture and, finally, to architecture.

59

81. Council on Foreign Relations, 58 East 68 Street at Park Avenue, 1920, by Delano & Aldrich. The Council on Foreign Relations is probably the most important of the private organizations concerned with the nation's foreign policy. The public knows of it because its magazine, *Foreign Affairs,* will on occasion contain an article that gains attention in the press.

The building was originally the Harold Pratt residence. He was the son of Charles Pratt, whose refining company was famous in its time for "Astral Oil." The company was merged with the Standard Oil Trust. He was also the founder of the Pratt Institute. Some of the family's mansions still stand on Clinton Street in Brooklyn.

With the development of Classical Park and Fifth Avenues on the Upper East Side, well-to-do Brooklyn families, among them the Pratts, were drawn to Manhattan.

What is particularly good about the facade is the treatment of the ground floor. It is not so much the rustication, a familiar device, as the handling of the fenestration. Sunken round, arched bays are set in the rusticated wall, and in the bay frames are found the windows. The glazing is also partly curved, reflecting the window's arch. The high second-floor windows indicate a *bel étage,* the rooms for entertaining. At the top, the attic has octagonal windows, and there is even a balustrade above the cornice. The style is eighteenth-century English, a favorite of Delano & Aldrich.

On the right there is an addition, designed to match the house, executed sometime later by the architect Frederick Rhinelander King.

82. The Frick Collection, 1 East 70 Street on Fifth Avenue, 1913–14, by Carrère & Hastings; 1935 (museum conversion), by John Russell Pope; 1977 (new addition), by John Barrington Bayley with G. Frederick Poehler and Harry Van Dyke. Terrace garden by Richard K. Webel; courtyard garden by Russell Page. The Frick Collection is the favorite art museum of many New Yorkers. It is small and presents objects of quality. The building itself adds much to the pleasure of the visitor.

Henry Clay Frick, the Pittsburgh coal-and-coke magnate, built it when his companies became part of the United States Steel Corporation and he moved to New York. It was not transformed into an art gallery until the 1930s, after the death of his widow. In the 1970s a new wing was added by the late John Barrington Bayley, a founder and first president of Classical America, the society which promotes the Classical tradition in American art.

Thomas Hastings was the architect of the original building, John Merven Carrère having died in 1911. Hastings looked, as he did often, to the French Classical for inspiration. The Ionic Order is not the favorite of Americans (the Corinthian is); it is not easy to handle. Here, where the Order takes the form of a pilaster on the main building, it is very successful. And it is on the wing that extends to the avenue along East 71 Street. A special Carrère & Hastings touch

exists in the pair of vases on the terrace steps. We think at once of the splendid vases in front of the portico of the New York Public Library.

The place given to sculpture on the facade on the Fifth Avenue wing and over the entrance on East 70 Street is noteworthy. The sculpture was designed by Sherry Edmundsen Fry, who studied at the Ecole. The carving was executed by the Piccirilli brothers, one of whom, Attilio, was responsible for the figures on the Maine Monument at Columbus Circle. (The brothers were *Carrarese*, sculptors from Carrara, Italy, who often did the actual stone carving for famous artists such as Daniel Chester French, who made the plaster models.) The wrought-iron fences and gate are particularly fine. The most recent part of the fence, that on the East 70 Street side, was made by Joseph Fiebiger.

The trustees of the Frick Collection deserve high praise for the pains taken in transforming the residence into a museum and then adding a wing. A measure of their care was their selecting a Classical architect and even seeing to it that the limestone came from the same quarry that furnished the stone of the original building. The Indiana Limestone Company of Bedford, Indiana, quarried the stone and had it carved in Bedford, following John Barrington Bayley's full-size blueprints.

83. Lycée Français (*left*, former Oliver Gould Jennings residence), **7 East 72 Street, 1899, by Ernest Flagg and Walter B. Chambers; Henry T. Sloane residence** (*right*), **9 East 72 Street, 1893–94, by Carrère & Hastings.** The architecture buff who is looking for the epitome of the Beaux-Arts will find it in these two buildings. The vermiculated rustication on the ground floor of No. 7, the elaborate foliated scroll frame with its cabochon over the entrance of No. 9 are very much what comes to mind when we think of Beaux-Arts as a style.

We scan the upper parts of both. Look at the French windows of the second floors of both residences, the leaves of the windows with their curved rails and the curved transoms. In the Jennings residence, the window bays, both sides and arch, have curved chamfering with a large scallop shell and garlands set in the arches. At the Sloane residence, the windows with their segmental arches have, in lieu of scallop shells, volutes with garlands. No. 9 triumphs in the two-story-high engaged columns with French Ionic capitals in the manner of Scamozzi.

When it comes to the roofs, No. 7 takes the lead. A curved mansard of slate and green copper flashing ends in an elaborate green copper crown. A student of Classical ornament can be pleasantly occupied in making out the details of the crown. Cabochons in scroll frames, cable molding, a lion mask, rinceaux in relief, these and others are present. If that is insufficient, there are the volutes, broken pediments, and cabochons of the dormer windows below. By comparison, the dormers of No. 9 are only modest.

No. 7 was built by William Brewster, the direct descendant of Deacon William Brewster, founder of the Plymouth Colony. William Brewster was the oldest of the original partners in the Standard Oil Trust. The house was a wedding present for his daughter. No. 9 was built by Henry T. Sloane, a member of the family that founded W. & J. Sloane, a store well known in its time for its home furnishings. The house was later the residence of James Stillman, the president of the National City Bank (today's Citicorp), who commissioned McKim, Mead & White to transform the old Merchants' Exchange building at 55 Wall Street into one of the finest banks in the city.

Today, both buildings belong to the Lycée Français, one of a number of schools that the French government maintains in cities around the world. The instruction is in French, the curriculum is that of a French *lycée* (secondary school) and, to graduate, students take the famous *bachot,* the baccalaureate exams.

84. Former Gertrude Rhinelander Waldo residence, 867 Madison Avenue at East 72 Street, 1898, by Kimball & Thompson. It is easy enough to understand the attraction of the châteaux of the Loire Valley in France, to which many travelers still make pilgrimages. They are beautiful, with a play of wall, fenestration and roofline, in varied settings that never lose appeal. Richard Morris Hunt introduced the fashion for these châteaux, a mixture of Late Gothic and Early Renaissance, to the city around 1880, and it lasted two decades. Here the inspiration would appear to be largely that of the

Château de Chambord, with its Gothic forms clothed in Renaissance detail. But the knowledgeable, no doubt, will find other models. Of all the mansion's features, nothing commands attention quite as much as the round-arched windows at the center of the avenue side. Such windows are common enough, but there are not many with the deep reveals. The fortress heritage of the rural, royal residences of the Loire was not lost in the transfer to New York. The roofline is very fine, a strong rival to that of the Warburg mansion farther north. The Gothic is found in the high-pitched roof of slate, the high, ornate dormers and the tall chimneys. The enrichment is early Renaissance, especially at the center dormers on both facades of the building, which boast colonnettes, broken entablatures, finials on high bases, finials in relief and volutes. In fact, although the dormers are ebullient, ornamentation is everywhere, even in the diamond-shaped pattern in relief on the chimneys (traceable to Chambord).

Once again we are astonished at how well served the architects of those days were by their craftsmen. Stone carving was a high art, possibly the noblest of the building trades. Who were these skilled craftsmen to whom New Yorkers owe so much? From what little we know, in the early 1880s most were English, some were German. Two decades later their number must have been supplemented by Italians and, no doubt, a few native sons. Two generations after the Waldo mansion was built, a ruthless shift in fashion in the arts led to the virtual disappearance of the craft.

85. Former Joseph Pulitzer residence, 11 East 73 Street, 1900–03, by McKim, Mead & White. It was fitting that Pulitzer, the great publisher of the *World,* should have a palace. He was hardly there for any length of time (with his eventual blindness and bouts of sickness, his chief refuge was his yacht *Liberty*), but it was his New York residence. Although Stanford White, representing the firm, found him no easy client, there was one moving episode in this client–architect struggle: White had to make a model of the facade for Pulitzer to judge by touch.

Several Venetian palaces served as inspiration, and possibly the Library of St. Mark, on the west side of the Piazzetta, opposite the Doge's Palace. The first floor is rusticated, even to the shafts of the columns at the entrance. The columns above are of the Scamozzi Order. Between the columns are arched windows with figures in the spandrels, in the Venetian manner. A Corinthian Order spans the third floor where the arched windows are somewhat smaller than those of the second floor. The frieze above the third floor has swags and plain panels. A cornice and a balustrade are at the top, the balustrade concealing an attic.

It is a splendid mansion. Close study reveals special touches, such as the different kinds of balusters (actually varieties of the double baluster). The balusters of the first-floor windows appear to be an invention of White's. What takes command is the superimposed rows of columns above the rusticated base. It is something of a surprise to come on such a house on a New York street. The formula White devised is a good one. Why did it not inspire imitations?

86. Cherokee Apartments, also known as East River Houses, East 77 Street and Cherokee Place at the East River Drive, 1909, by Henry Atterbury Smith. One of the canards tossed at the Beaux-Arts generation was that its architects catered only to the wealthy and neglected the needs of the working class. (Art historians, continuing to mock the great patrons of architecture at the turn of the century, seem to be incapable of recognizing that the wealthy—the Vanderbilts, the Astors, the Goelets, the Whitneys and others—made grand architecture possible. Without their patronage, there would have been no architects worth the title.) The fact is that architects, if not their rich clients, often pleaded for low-income housing. In the 1870s, Richard Morris Hunt pointed out what had been done by Napoleon III in encouraging such housing in the Second Empire. Admittedly, there was more discussion than action, but it is only fair to credit them with concern. Among the vocal element was Ernest Flagg who, in the 1890s, backed up his plea with designs.

One consequence of his efforts was the Cherokee Apartments, built with the backing of Mrs. William Kissam Vanderbilt. It is most suitably sited, overlooking the East River next to John Jay Park. It consists of a block of four buildings between East 77 and East 78 Streets, each built around a small court. The apartments would be called "utility" today, although somewhat larger than what the label conveys, for they had several rooms, a kitchen and a bathroom.

The yellow brick and limestone facade was given a curious treatment. The ornament is recognizably of Classical origin, but so short on enrichment that it recalls the Secessionism of Vienna 1900. Everything is flat and squared off, not unlike the work of Frank Lloyd Wright, who was very much a Secessionist. The tone is one of sternness, as if the dwellers in these modest apartments deserved no more.

87. Cultural Services of the French Embassy, 972 Fifth Avenue, (*right*), 1902–06, by McKim, Mead & White. 973 Fifth Avenue (*left*), 1902–05, by McKim, Mead & White. These houses by the great firm, although seeming to be of one design, were actually separate ventures. It is No. 972 that commands our interest. It was built by Oliver Payne, partner in the Standard Oil Trust, for his nephew Payne Whitney, and the latter's bride, Helen Hay Whitney. (Payne Whitney was the son of William Collins Whitney and Helen Hay was the daughter of John Hay, President McKinley's Secretary of State. Payne Whitney, heir to a vast fortune, was an outstanding philanthropist. Among his important beneficiaries were Yale University, the Metropolitan Museum of Art, New York Hospital and the New York Public Library. John Hay Whitney and Mrs. Charles Shipman Payson, first owner of the Mets, were his children.)

Experts see the inspiration as being the Pesaro Palace on Venice's Grand Canal, but the game of identifying sources of a Stanford White building can be endless. At least it is pleasant that there is more than one building on the avenue linking the Queen of the Hudson and the Queen of the Adriatic.

The identifying elements are the pairs of Ionic pilasters (columns on the Venetian palace) of the second floor which frame round-arch windows. The figures in the arch spandrels are another Venetian touch. Still, Fifth Avenue is a long way away from the Grand Canal; the interpretation is free. Particularly nice touches are the masks and fruit garlands over the third-floor windows and the marble figure reliefs above the fourth-floor windows. These last must have an eighteenth-century provenance, probably French.

Occasionally, the French Embassy has exhibitions here, and the public is admitted to the ground floor. It is well worth a visit to see the interior.

88

88. New York University Institute of Fine Arts (former James B. Duke mansion), 1 East 78 Street on Fifth Avenue, 1912, by Horace Trumbauer. For a man who, in his lifetime, was looked down on by the profession (he was not admitted to the American Institute of Architects until the end of his career), Horace Trumbauer left an elegant imprint, much of which survives, on New York and his native Philadelphia (*see also* remarks on Wildenstein Gallery). This mansion, the best known of his New York houses, was built for James Buchanan Duke, the North Carolinian who made his money in tobacco and electricity. Much of his fortune went to Duke University, whose beautiful campus in Durham, North Carolina, was designed by Trumbauer. Duke's widow and his daughter Doris gave the beautiful building to New York University in 1957.

For his model, Trumbauer turned, as he did so often, to an eighteenth-century French model—in this instance the Hôtel Labottière in Bordeaux. (It was this unabashed appropriation of French designs that so annoyed his fellow architects.) What Trumbauer did seems simple enough: He changed the proportions and a few details. The changes may appear simple, but few architects

have possessed Trumbauer's ability to achieve a design that is both fitting for a New York street and superior to the original source of inspiration.

The facade is severe, its chief distinction being the unusual windows on both floors. Between the windows are large, flat panels. A horizontal member in the form of a deep stringcourse separates the two floors. To grasp how important this course is, try to imagine the facade without it. The only ornamentation are the flower swags and rosettes over the second-floor windows.

The severe wings make the entrance, marked by its own sobriety, all the more effective. Rusticated sides establish the double recess of the doorway and second-floor bay. A double pair of columns, Doric at the entrance and Scamozzi Ionic above, provide an accent. The whole is crowned by a pediment. At ground level, balustrades border the sunken area. They are also in the first-story windows and top the cornice, where they conceal a raised roof and give a sense of scale. The net result is monumentality in what is, for New York, a low building.

65

89. Ukrainian Institute of America, 2 East 79 Street at Fifth Avenue, 1899, by C. P. H. Gilbert. Richard Morris Hunt, with his design for William Kissam Vanderbilt's residence at 660 Fifth Avenue, set the fashion for late Gothic–early Renaissance French architecture. It seemed to be the style favored by wealth wanting a substantial presence in the city, especially on Fifth Avenue.

As with so many of these private houses, even the large ones, it was built for an unknown—Isaac D. Fletcher, a coal-mine owner from Ohio. From 1921 to 1929, it was occupied by Harry T. Sinclair, one of the several oil men involved in the Teapot Dome scandal. Through Albert Fall, Secretary of the Interior in the Harding cabinet, he had obtained leases to the Naval oil reserves at Teapot Dome, Wyoming. He refused to testify at the Senate hearings, for which he was held in contempt of Congress and was sent to jail from this house.

The final private owner was Augustus Van Horn Stuyvesant, the last of Pegleg's descendants. When he died in 1953, his remains were removed from here and buried in the churchyard of St. Mark's-in-the-Bowery.

The Gothic takes many shapes here. The depressed three-centered arch at the entrance and the pseudo-three-centered arch above it are a fair sample of the arches, which include, as well, the round and the pointed. But it is in the detail that the style proclaims itself: The tracery with its cusping of the second-floor window over the entrance and, at one window of the third floor, the corbel table at the cornice and, above all, the finials. But there are also the crouching dwarfs, Atlases with globes and seated lions with shields found at the entrance.

90. Center Facade, Metropolitan Museum of Art, Fifth Avenue and East 82 Street, 1893-1902, by Richard Morris Hunt and Richard Howland Hunt. The monumentality, the disposition of the three wide bays with the paired Corinthian columns, the high attic and the silhouette of female masks set against scallop shells confirm that the architects of this part of the museum had been in Paris. Richard Morris Hunt was, in fact, the first American architect to come out of the Ecole, which his oldest son, Paris-born Richard Howland, was later to attend.

In the early 1890s, the elder Hunt had been asked for a plan for an expanded museum, along with an elevation for a new center facade. He had hardly presented his designs in 1895 when he died. With the trustees' approval, Richard Howland stepped in and carried the work to completion.

A glance at the Roosevelt Building on lower Broadway shows that, at the museum, we are a long way from Richard Morris' early work. Except for the base of the Statue of Liberty, nearly all of what he designed in the city has disappeared. It is strange that the man who transformed Fifth Avenue—if only for little more than a generation—should be represented in New York by the museum and not by one of his great private palaces, which can be seen only at Newport, Rhode Island.

Here Hunt produced an imperial facade. On a rusticated base he placed four pairs of Corinthian columns and three round-arched bays, the center one serving as entrance. What makes the columns supremely effective is that they support massive broken entablatures. Above and behind them is a high attic with a cornice that carries the row of female masks. Attics can have a deadening quality when their horizontality is not broken, as it is here by the entablatures. In addition, the row of masks brings needed enrichment.

Also breaking the horizontal effect are uncut blocks of stone on the tops of the entablatures. The two Hunts had intended to have them cut into sculptural groups representing the arts. The museum trustees demurred at the proposal. So, in an attempt to force their hand, Richard Howland Hunt placed the blocks on the entablatures expecting that, eventually, they would be carved.

Museum buildings of the Beaux-Arts era, unlike those of today, were decorated with sculpture. At the Metropolitan, Karl Bitter did the relief portraits in the arch spandrels, the standing figures on the short wings to either side of the column front and was to have been the sculptor of the uncut blocks.

The present flight of steps dates from 1970. Originally there was a much smaller flight concentrated at the center bay, making the rusticated base more conspicuous and the general impression of the facade more monumental. The present steps, while more practical, have altered the artistic aspect of the entrance.

91. Cooper-Hewitt Museum, The Smithsonian Institution's National Museum of Design (former Andrew Carnegie mansion), 2 East 91 Street, 1899–1902, by Babb, Cook & Willard. In many ways this mansion might qualify as more "American" than most of the other surviving mansions in the city. The combination of the dark red brick with the bold trim of Indiana limestone and the glass-and-bronze porte cochere of the entrance can still be found in such other American cities as St. Louis, Washington and Chicago. To call it "more American" is simply to say that its inspiration is not identifiable, whereas a house by Horace Trumbauer can be traced to a particular French model. But Trumbauer, in adapting the model to a New York street, changed certain details and transformed the proportions to the point where it is very much his building, an American building. This is a game which is probably better left to writers of doctoral theses in art history.

Of the firm little is known, except that it also did the De Vinne Press Building on Lafayette and West 4 Streets. One of the partners, George Fletcher "Badger" Babb, had been a colleague of Charles Follen McKim in the office of the New York and Chicago architect Peter B. Wight.

From this house, where Andrew Carnegie lived in the last decades of his life, the magnate gave away the millions he had made in coal, iron and steel. While his name survives in several institutes and foundations, he is best remembered for having given some $4.5 million for 1679 public libraries in the United States alone, of which New York City was the chief beneficiary.

The interior reflects the man. The museum has very wisely kept as much of the paneling and other decoration as possible. The visitor should pause in the foyer on entering; on the wall to the left are photographs of the various rooms showing how they were furnished in the great man's day.

There is a garden occupying half the lot; the big house on the open lot is very much in the American tradition, as we know from surviving portions of residential avenues in the nation's older cities. At one point there were a number of such mansions on the avenue, but they soon disappeared; only this and that of the Frick Collection, built by Andrew Carnegie's one-time partner, are still with us.

92. The Jewish Museum, 1109 Fifth Avenue at East 92 Street, 1907–08, by Charles P. H. Gilbert. The building is one of the Gothic (late French Gothic, to be exact) mansions that survive on the avenue. Only 13 blocks to the south is another, the Ukrainian Institute at East 79 Street.

The impression is of a building executed in a style wholly foreign to us today. Yet, for all the strangeness of the style, it was designed with consummate ease. Gilbert had to his credit a number of such mansions, not all of them Gothic. He took his cue for the style, as did other architects, from Richard Morris Hunt's William Kissam Vanderbilt residence, which stood at the northwest corner of Fifth Avenue and West 52 Street.

Those knowledgeable in the style might point to the house of Jacques Cœur in Bourges and the Palace of Justice in Rouen as the ancestors of the building. But the interpretation is free, and it is severe when compared to the style of its ancestors.

The fenestration is one of the mansion's conspicuous features, not just in size but also in the variety of arched openings. The round arch found in some of the windows is familiar enough, but not the three-centered ones of the wide windows of the second floor, of the fourth floor and of the end gables at the top. On the third floor, the central window has a depressed three-centered arch as does the entrance. In the three dormers over the center, the window arches are segmental.

The Gothic note is fully underscored by the projections over the windows (called, variously, dripstones, dripmolds or hood molds). Those of the wide windows of the second floor have central finials in relief. Not least is the richly varied Gothic roof topped by wispy metal finials and dormers with high gables with crockets and finials. Inside, many rooms remain unchanged.

The building was commissioned by Felix Moritz Warburg of the great banking family of Hamburg, Germany. Instead of joining the family firm of M. M. Warburg & Company, he went to work in Frankfurt, met and married Frieda Schiff, daughter of Jacob H. Schiff, and became a partner in his father-in-law's firm, Kuhn, Loeb & Company. While active in the business, he was best known as head of the family philanthropies, notably the Federation of Jewish Philanthropies of New York, of which he was a founder.

93. Former William Goadby Loew–Billy Rose residence, 56 East 93 Street between Park and Madison Avenues, 1931, by Walker & Gillette. No. 56 was the last of the mansions to be built in New York. Fashion had changed; persons of means had come to live in large apartments. William Goadby Loew, the son-in-law of the great banker George F. Baker, was an exception. He wanted a house, but lived in it for only a short while. The residence was later owned by Billy Rose, the successful theatrical producer in the 1930s. A high point of his career was the Aquacade at the 1939 New York World's Fair.

Walker & Gillette created a 1920s version of the work of Robert Adam, the Scotsman who was the bright light of English architecture in the latter half of the eighteenth century. Such adaptations were more common in interior decoration. The center portion of the house, with its sides curving into wings, and the rippling outer surface of the arch of the Palladian windows of the wings, give the twentieth-century Adamesque flavor. A more familiar device is the Vitruvian wave or scroll on a band running along the top of the facade. The distinctive aedicule at the entrance belongs to an older tradition. Its columns are of the Composite Order, rarely found in this country (this may well be the only example of it in the city). A combination of Ionic and Corinthian, the Composite was very popular in Rome during the Baroque era.

94. International Center of Photography (former Willard Straight residence), 1130 Fifth Avenue at East 94 Street, 1913–15, by Delano & Aldrich. There is a certain sober, subdued touch in the work of Delano & Aldrich. It is found in their Greenwich House in Greenwich Village, in the headquarters of the Russian Orthodox Church Outside of Russia at Park Avenue and East 93 Street, and in the private houses now occupied by St. David's School at 12 East 89 Street. Nowhere is their touch better exemplified than here, where it lies in the use of a good red brick and marble (rather than the customary limestone) trim. It is the firm's favorite style, English Georgian, treated severely.

At the ground floor, the windows are small, and even the doorway is modest, although it has a pair of engaged Tuscan columns. As always in these houses, the accent is on the second story, where the tall windows extend to the floor. The otherwise simple facade at this point has as a modest accent the window over the entrance with a stone frame and pediment. The round windows at the top are a Delano & Aldrich signature, although at the Council of Foreign Relations their shape is octagonal rather than round.

The client of the firm for this house was Willard Straight, who married a daughter of William Collins Whitney. Best remembered as the founding publisher of *The New Republic*, he was the father of the actress Beatrice Straight. Subsequent owners were Judge Gary of the United States Steel Corporation and Mrs. Harrison Williams, who here held one of the city's more fashionable salons of the 1930s.

95. Congregation Shearith Israel, 8 West 70 Street on Central Park West, 1897, by Brunner & Tryon. Although his name is not widely known, Arnold Brunner left his mark on the city in a striking way. The public bath on East 23 Street is his, reflecting the talent of a man who had a solid command of the Classical vocabulary and was not afraid to make full use of it.

Admittedly, this temple for the city's oldest Jewish congregation—it is Sephardic—is severe. The inspiration could be said to be Greek, if we look first at the attic and the pediment with the three acroteria. But then the eye is caught by the Corinthian columns—essentially Roman. In addition to joining the Greek and the Roman, he has four columns on four high bases set on a flight of steps, a Renaissance touch, as are the balustrades at the three tall windows over the three entrances.

A Greek temple would have had figures in the pediment. They cannot be used here because the Jewish religion is iconoclastic. Instead, we find an oculus in a wreath frame set between two rinceaux carved in bold relief.

As with so many of New York's Beaux-Arts structures, the interior is not to be ignored. The hall, if plain, is monumental and very fine. There is, in addition, a surprise: the reproduction of the interior of the congregation's (and the city's) first synagogue building (1730) at the back of the hall. Having a number of ancient objects that were in the original building, it conveys a charming note of the Colonial city as well as serving as contrast to Brunner's synagogue.

96. The Dakota, 1 West 72 Street on Central Park West, 1884, by Henry Janeway Hardenbergh. Certain New York architects have been fortunate in having their work survive more than a generation. Such a one is Henry Janeway Hardenbergh (1847–1918), whose name, by the way, is to be seen in the nave of St. Bartholomew's Church. His work survives in the Plaza Hotel, the Art Students League and the former Hotel Albert on University Place, as well as in the Copley Plaza Hotel in Boston and the Willard Hotel in Washington. (His biggest commission, the old Waldorf-Astoria, is gone. It stood on the site of the Empire State Building.)

The Dakota is one of the city's great apartment buildings. Edward S. Clark of the Singer Sewing Machine Company commissioned Hardenbergh to design it for the then-burgeoning West Side. With the breakup of the old estates in that part of the city and the end of the

depression of the 1870s, the West Side grew and, for a decade or so, enjoyed a moment of fashion.

The building, which originally had 85 apartments, is constructed around a large interior court. Each apartment was designed as if it were a private residence, only with all the rooms on one floor. The double parlor of the old New York row house was found here. Initially there were rooms for common use such as a laundry, a kitchen and a dining room; transient guests were welcome. For long, at least on the West Side, it stood for the epitome of comfortable middle-class living. In the 1930s many from the world of the theater came to live in it, and the aura of the world of entertainment is still present.

The style of the building is a mixture of the French Renaissance and the Gothic. Modified oriels are on the street side, in this instance

They stretch from the second floor to the top of the facade, ending in octagonal domes. There are empty niches with balconies and semidomes. These devices, along with the finials at the top of the gables with their step roofs, underscore the Gothic note. Fanciers of the Renaissance will be rewarded by the splendid cast-iron masks of the railing along the sidewalk.

97. The Dorilton, 171 West 71 Street at Broadway, 1902, by Janes & Leo. High mansards were at one time very much part of Broadway. They were once clustered around Times Square, where only one, that of the old Knickerbocker Hotel, has survived. A few remain at West 72 Street and farther north, making a strong imprint on the thoroughfare.

The Dorilton has all the opulence of ornament that is so much part of the turn of the century. The bold rustication, the massive brackets of the fourth-floor cornice (also seen higher up, where the original cornice and balustrades have been removed), the entrance with its posts topped by globes, the bridge spanning the space between the two wings on the street side—all create a cumulative effect crowned by the mansard, which has managed to retain its elaborate cresting and tall chimneys.

The Dorilton is a striking building in its sheer abundance of ornament, including a pair of statues at the center of the fourth floor on the Broadway side, easily seen from the sidewalk. Anonymous work, they are in the manner of Jean Goujon, the great sixteenth-century French sculptor.

98

98 & 99. The Ansonia Hotel, Broadway and West 73 Street, 1899–1904, by W. E. D. Stokes and Graves & Duboy. It is astonishing how few foreign architects practiced in this country during the great era of our architecture. This is particularly true when compared to our own times. The best known was E. L. Masqueray, who designed the Roman Catholic cathedrals of St. Paul and Minneapolis. Equally rare were the instances in which foreign firms were invited to design single buildings. René Sergent of Paris worked with Horace Trumbauer on the long-gone Duveen Building. There is also the example of Jacques Gréber, another Parisian, who executed formal gardens for the Wideners and the Stotesburys and laid out Philadelphia's Franklin Parkway. Gertrude Jekyll of England is credited with several gardens in Connecticut. In the Ansonia, we have the example of a developer, W. E. D. Stokes, calling on a French firm, Graves & Duboy, to do the design. The building is credited to all three.

There is no doubt about the Beaux-Arts influence here. It is not just that the architects were French. The style is French, stemming from Charles Garnier, the architect of the Paris Opéra and the casino at Monte Carlo. What is American is the size. The mansard roof, two stories high, with its elaborate single and double dormers, is spectacular. At the corners are domes with strange crowns—drums that served as platforms for cupolas that disappeared over the years. A high, elaborate tower planned for the center of the building was left unbuilt.

99

The distinguishing parts of the facade are the curved corners rising to the domes. They and the rest of the facade were given a superabundance of ornament. The brackets are awesome; those at the principal cornice-balcony might be described as gigantic—in a building of this size they have to be. Although the Broadway front at ground level has been altered for commercial use, the street side remains relatively unchanged. The architecture buff is urged to go there to obtain a close look at some of the detail. At the entrance is a massive pediment consisting of two volutes joined at the middle by a scroll frame, small volutes and an elaborate scallop shell. The large volutes rest on entablatures with pulvinated friezes with well-rounded surfaces. The Order here is a French Scamozzi Ionic. The collector of examples of Classical ornament in the city should make certain that this entrance is on his list.

The Ansonia was (and remains) popular with the world of the theater and entertainment. For a number of years, the great Flo Ziegfeld and his wife, Billie Burke, lived here.

100. Apple Bank for Savings (former Central Savings Bank), 2100 Broadway at West 73 Street, 1928, by York & Sawyer. New Yorkers can be forgiven if they do not know of the once-strong German presence in the city. World War I brought a hysterical effort to wipe out any trace of it, reinforced by World War II and the Holocaust. Still, the fact remains that no satisfactory history of the city can be written without acknowledging the key role that Germans, both Christian and Jewish, have had in shaping it. In banking, we think of (among the better-known) Jacob Schiff and the Warburgs, but the German influence was felt everywhere, from music publishing to breweries. The Central Savings Bank, for example, was originally the Germania Savings Bank, just as Lenox Hill Hospital was once the German Hospital.

The Beaux-Arts era was the great age of bank buildings, such as this one. Many are gone, but some survive. Among the architects prominent in their design was the firm of York & Sawyer. Of the two men, Edward Palmer York and Philip Sawyer, the latter was the designer of the firm. They met when draftsmen in the office of McKim, Mead & White. Their most important building in the city is the Federal Reserve Bank downtown. As he did with that great fortress, Sawyer turned to Florence for inspiration, as can be guessed from the Tuscan arch of the windows and the use of rustication from the ground to the main cornice (similar to the Federal Reserve Bank). The first story serves as base. It is very effective partly because the channeling of the rustication makes the blocks of limestone appear larger than the ones above. But it is the handling of the large windows, with their Tuscan arches, that gives a special rhythm to the rusticated wall. At the top of the facade there are two-story-high bays separated by rusticated walls with Tuscan pilasters.

The nice touches of York & Sawyer are there: the pair of lions over the main entrance, the elaborate scroll frame at the keystone of the arch above and, on the side at about the same height, a stone plaque with scroll frame, shields and swags.

The building's elegance is carried into the interior, with wrought iron by Samuel Yellin. The chairman of the old Central Savings was, for a number of years, James T. Lee, the maternal grandfather of Mrs. Jacqueline Onassis. He and Charles Russell Fleischmann were responsible for McKim, Mead & White's 998 Fifth Avenue, one of New York's finest apartment houses. Lee had unerring taste in architecture, and we can feel certain that York & Sawyer's work drew him here as much as solid business reasons.

101. Theodore Roosevelt Memorial at the American Museum of Natural History, Central Park West between West 77 Street and West 81 Street, 1936, by John Russell Pope. It does seem odd that a great American president should be commemorated, in the city of his birth and where his political career began, by a wing of a museum. Nevertheless, it is here, part of one of the great scientific museums of the world. In its displays, dioramas, collections and research facilities, it is unrivaled.

The facade is almost a triumphal arch, with pairs of tall Ionic columns on a high base setting off the entrance. Between the pairs is a high arch with an admirable keystone of an eagle on a volute. Above the columns is an entablature broken at four points to carry four statues of American heroes in the exploration of nature: Daniel

Boone, James J. Audubon, William Clark and Meriwether Lewis (of the Lewis and Clark Expedition). They are the work of James Earle Fraser. The columns, broken entablatures and statues are very effective; together they make for an accent on needed verticality. In addition, the statues bring visual relief to the high attic which, if they were not present, would appear too heavy and too bare. The animal reliefs on the terrace walls are the work of James L. Clark.

It is praiseworthy that, in its sculpture, this science museum bids welcome to the arts. And praise must also go to the equestrian statue of our twenty-sixth president (also by Fraser). One of the failures of contemporary architecture is absence of sculpture, certainly sculpture of any meaning. Its presence here is one of the major contributions of the influence of the Beaux-Arts.

102

102. Apthorp Apartments, 2207 Broadway at West 79 Street, 1908, by Clinton & Russell. The Apthorp is one of the city's great apartment buildings, but being on the Upper West Side (unfashionable until recently), it is less well known than its equivalents on the East Side. For one thing, it is bigger than most, occupying the whole block from Broadway to West End Avenue and from West 78 to West 79 Streets.

The entrance has great character. Two pairs of Corinthian pilasters frame it, attesting to the decorative quality of the Order. The arched entrance, leading to a large interior court, has admirable decoration in the helmeted mask on the keystone and the graceful figures in the spandrels. At the fourth floor, above the entablature, are four female figures in full relief. Like those in the spandrels, they are beautifully executed; an unknown did this work, which is as good as that to be found anywhere in the country. We owe the figures

probably to one of the anonymous skilled sculptors who did the actual carving for such well-known men as Daniel Chester French or Frederick MacMonnies. This assumption is based on the fact that the craftsmen-sculptors (or journeymen-sculptors) did Classical works, as found here, whereas the well-known sculptors were caught up in realism. A craftsman-sculptor, for example, would have been responsible for the two panels between the figures which have reliefs of decorated posts holding flaming urns.

The building takes its name from Charles Ward Apthorp, the owner of an eighteenth-century house that stood nearby. In the 1870s, during the breakup of the West Side estates that had been country places, the property was bought by John Jacob Astor III, whose son, William Waldorf Astor, founded the English branch of the family. The latter's estate (managed separately from the American branch) built the apartment house.

103. First Church of Christ, Scientist, 1 West 96 Street at Central Park West, 1903, by Carrère & Hastings. The Christian Science Church, like many churches of the Evangelical Protestants and like many synagogues, does not have images. Christian Scientists are iconoclasts. This has not prevented them from turning to the Classical tradition, where they have made full use of a number of ancient devices. Probably the most elaborate Christian Science church in the city is this one. The first impression is of great severity, in part due to the gray granite that clads the facade. The bare walls flanking the central block also offer a slightly forbidding touch. Otherwise, the facade has movement in its devices and ornament.

Let us scan the motifs that take away something of the severity. The entrance has a pair of columns with shafts made of alternating drums, fluted and smooth. The doorway has a square-arched top with a volute on the keystone. The entrance is actually part of a high central bay framed by Ionic columns. Between the columns is a high secondary bay having a frame of rustication and curved chamfering derived from the French Classical. Inside the second bay is a tall window. This mixture of column, chamfered and rusticated sides and a tall window (over a pedimented entrance) make for a play of light and shadow of different shapes that is very effective.

Over the central block is a tower equally imposing and equally novel. Its base is square-sided with tall round-arched windows on all four sides. Framing the windows are engaged Ionic columns with entablature and pediments. A low, square attic with corner quoins rises behind the pediments. Then, as a surprise, four large flaming urns stand at the four corners, making a startling effect. The eight-sided steeple, also of granite, rises, not to a spire but to a blunt end, as if it also served as a chimney.

Altogether the congregation has an astonishing house of worship.

104. Former New York Cancer Hospital, 2 West 106 Street at Central Park West, 1887, by Charles C. Haight. Charles C. Haight is best known for the chapel and most of the buildings of the General Theological Seminary on Ninth Avenue and West 20 Street. They form a pleasant Gothic campus in what is known as Chelsea Square. Four miles to the north is this châteaulike structure in what might be termed late French Gothic, a variation of the style that was the architect's specialty. This is a long way away from today's imposing hospitals, with their many stories and lengthy corridors. No doubt the old New York Cancer Hospital was not the paradigm of efficiency we would expect today, but there is an attraction in its size and in its design, which has character.

Perhaps the label of Plain Medieval might serve, since the building's distinguishing feature is the presence of two round, stubby towers with cone-shaped slate roofs. The arches, of course, could qualify as Romanesque, but by the end of the Gothic era the ogive was competing with the round arch. It is seen in the arcades with short columns and Gothic capitals. The round arch is repeated in the dormers, which are framed by engaged columns with short finials and rise to gables, also with finials.

The materials are humble enough: Philadelphia pressed brick and brownstone, no doubt from Portland in the Connecticut Valley. Both materials, so popular in the Civil War era, continued in use into this century.

The old building, a nursing home at one point, figured in the nursing-home scandal of the 1970s. There are plans to convert it to residential use.

103

105. Low Library, Columbia University, Broadway and West 116 Street, 1895–98, by McKim, Mead & White. The Columbia University campus, with Low Library at its center, was probably the work of which Charles Follen McKim was most proud. After Thomas Jefferson's University of Virginia in Charlottesville, it is the finest Classical campus in the country. The scheme is simplicity itself: Buildings of the same materials (brick and limestone), of similar height and in a similar Classical manner, are set around a rectangle on a series of terraces. At the center of the court formed in this fashion is the domed Low Library, which dominates the whole scheme.

The eye begins here with the series of flights of steps and terraces rising from College Walk (West 116 Street) that are embellished with fountains and urns. In the middle of one flight is the statue of Alma Mater by Daniel Chester French. The last flight of steps is framed by two cheek walls on which are a pair of bronze lamp standards copied from an ancient one in marble in the Vatican Museum. Then comes the porch, with its ten Greek Ionic columns and, over it, an attic.

Behind the attic, an octagonal drum carries a low dome, inspired by that of the Pantheon. The detail of the exterior is a mixture of Roman and Greek, as often happened with similar monumental buildings in the Beaux-Arts era. The same mixture is carried into the interior, where a rotunda has splendid Ionic columns and where the high surrounding halls have ceilings with deep coffering filled with rosettes.

This grand setting is a major attraction on a sunny day. In clement weather, when the university is in session, the steps are crowded with students. The color and movement, along with the sparkle of the fountains, make for a wonderful urban spectacle.

New Yorkers have honored architects in many ways. There is the stained-glass window in St. Patrick's depicting James Renwick showing his plans for the cathedral to the archbishop. Across from the Frick Collection there is a monument to Richard Morris Hunt. At Columbia an inscription in bronze letters in the pavement of one of the terraces is dedicated to McKim. It is well deserved.

104

PRESENTED BY
THE CLASS OF 1885 COLVMBIA COLLEGE
ON THEIR TWENTY-FIFTH ANNIVERSARY
JVNE 1 1910

105

106. Brooklyn Museum, Eastern Parkway and Washington Avenue, Brooklyn, 1893-1915, by McKim, Mead & White. Art museums became important in the Beaux-Arts era, the example having been set by Charles Atwood's Palace of Fine Arts (built for the Chicago World's Columbian Exposition of 1893) which was reborn in the 1930s as the Museum of Science and Industry. As a form of a city's embellishment, part of what was called the "City Beautiful Movement," the movers and the shakers felt that there had to be a majestic building devoted to the arts. Uppermost in their minds was not only the education of the public, but the education and training of the artist. Art museums often had schools or were affiliated with art schools and housed large collections of casts that aspirants drew in studying the antique. And aspirants, in continuing their apprenticeship, also copied pictures. Some museums even boasted murals, such as the Boston Museum of Fine Arts with its works by Sargent, and sculpture, which can be seen at the Metropolitan Museum of Art in the work of Karl Bitter. In the Brooklyn Museum it is overwhelmingly sculpture, executed by Daniel Chester French, Adolph A. Weinman, George T. Brewster, Kenyon Cox, Herbert Adams, John Gelert, Carl A. Heber, Edward Clark Potter, Attilio Piccirilli, Edmond T. Quinn, Charles Keck, Augustus Lukeman and Janet Scudder. Few other buildings can boast of such an array, unless it be the Library of Congress or the Appellate Court on Madison Square. This is true patronage—inviting the artist to decorate a public building (which, as the French painter Ingres observed, is the artist's highest responsibility).

The Brooklyn Museum is also to be praised for its beautiful building. McKim, Mead & White obtained the commission in 1893 as a result of a competition. The original design was for a much larger structure, 560 feet square with four interior courts. At its center it was to have a dome on a high drum. As it turned out, only one side was built in full, that on Eastern Parkway, and half a side on Washington

Avenue. The low saucer dome seen here is simply part of the one side; there were to be four altogether along with the larger central one on the drum.

While the scale is Roman, the style is predominantly Greek, as can be seen in the use of a Greek Ionic Order for the porch antefixes and acroteria on the cresting of the attics and the raking cornices of the central pediment. The dome is Roman. The pediment is filled with sculpture by Daniel Chester French and Adolph A. Weinman.

Unfinished as it is, the Brooklyn Museum is a magnificent building. For that reason it is sad to recall that it was badly manhandled in the 1930s. A disaster befell it in 1936, when the imperial flight of steps leading to the portico was removed—a mutilation that is to be remedied by the restoration of the steps. A new addition, in the Modernistic style, is currently planned for the museum.

107. Soldiers' and Sailors' Monument, Grand Army Plaza at the juncture of Eastern Parkway, Flatbush Avenue and the entrance to Prospect Park, Brooklyn, 1892, by John H. Duncan, with sculpture by Philip Martiny and Frederick MacMonnies. The Soldiers' and Sailors' Monument is the finest triumphal arch of modern times, second only to the Arc de Triomphe in Paris.

What makes a triumphal arch effective is the presence of sculpture. The arch is nothing other than a useful pedestal for the sculptor, a fact amply proved by the Soldiers' and Sailors' Monument. (An arch without sculpture, without ornament, without detail, is not a true arch but an exercise in construction.)

John H. Duncan, who was the architect of Grant's Tomb, won the competition for the arch design in 1889. When first built, it had no sculpture and looked very severe. Fortunately, in the 1890s, the city of Brooklyn obtained one of the outstanding park commissioners in the city's history, a successful paper manufacturer named Frank Squier.

He commissioned Frederick MacMonnies, the Brooklyn-born sculptor, to execute a quadriga (a four-horse chariot) with figures for the summit and two groups, *Army* on the left, *Navy* on the right, for the side facing the park. For all his realism (realism, also called naturalism, had, as a result of French influence, come to dominate American sculpture and painting), MacMonnies produced works of art of vitality with figures and composition along Classical lines. (This realism has nothing to do with today's realism, which is ugly or brutal, or both.) In the *Army* and *Navy* groups, the figures are packed in with clustered rifles, goddesses of war, falling horses, guns and other military hardware—all to spectacular effect.

Part of the impression the arch makes comes from its setting on the park side, with Doric columns bearing bronze eagles on globes and other features added in the 1890s by Stanford White. Even in an age in which car and truck traffic has taken over grand settings, the arch and its setting still dominate.

In addition to the MacMonnies work on the arch, there are the spandrel figures by Philip Martiny and, inside the arch on the abutments, reliefs of an equestrian Lincoln and an equestrian Grant by Thomas Eakins and William O'Donovan. Unfortunately, these bronze panels, where horse and man are less than life-size, are wholly out of scale.

Standing at the entrance to Prospect Park looking north at the arch, the spectator sees one of the nation's great works of art. The brio of the two groups, especially that of *Army*, and the splendid figures and horses of the quadriga are breathtaking.

108. Museum Building, The New York Botanical Garden, The Bronx, 1902, by Robert W. Gibson. For the visitor on his first trip to the New York Botanical Garden, the Museum Building is almost bewildering. What is such a structure doing in a botanical garden? A large structure was needed to house an herbarium, library, offices and other facilities of a great institution, as well as to provide space for exhibitions. In the Beaux-Arts era, even if such a building were to be set in a park (and at the time it was well beyond the built-up portion of the city), it had to be majestic.

Its site was suitable to that end because it offered a gentle slope as an approach, making for a greater sense of monumentality, also created by the long flight of steps and the high Corinthian columns, but there was no harm in having an extra fillip to increase the sensation of height. The broken entablatures above the columns were obviously intended to serve as bases for statues, much as they do at the Roosevelt Memorial of the American Museum of Natural History. Often the architect is blamed for not inviting the help of the sculptor, but it could well have been the trustees who were not interested. At least, Robert W. Gibson did have the satisfaction of seeing the city's seal placed over the entrance and a second one at the center of the attic.

We should not be too hasty in rebuking the trustees, because they commissioned Carl E. Tefft to do the fountain at the foot of the steps. It is a wonderful spectacle of seahorses being reined in by boys.

The New York Botanical Garden, like the Brooklyn Botanic Garden, is one of those city resources that the public takes for granted. Perhaps because it is not in the city's center, perhaps because flowers are not displayed everywhere as in England or Holland, for whatever reason, New Yorkers pass it by. With the newly restored Enid Haupt Conservatory, with the exhibitions in the Museum Building, with plantations and gardens—especially the rock garden—with the new rose garden, along with its scientific research and instruction, the Botanical Garden is one of New York's treasures. Currently there are plans to enlarge the building.

GLOSSARY

Abacus. See diagram.

Acanthus. A Mediterranean plant, stylized in Classical architecture to provide ornament, especially in the capital of the Corinthian and Composite Orders.

Acroterion. An ornament placed at the corner or peak of a roof or pediment.

Aedicule. A small frame or house suggesting a Classical temple.

Ancone. A bracket in scroll form, usually supporting a cornice above a door or window.

Antefix. An upright ornament, frequently of an anthemion design, in the eaves of a Classical building, originally intended to hide the ends of a row of tiles.

Anthemion. Ornamentation based on the stylized palm leaf or honeysuckle.

Antis, in. Usually used to describe columns standing between the antae (extensions of the side walls), rather than in front of them.

Arabesque. An intricate pattern that incorporates plant and animal forms.

Architrave. See diagram.

Ashlar. Building stones that have been cut square.

Attic. The story constructed above a building's cornice.

Balustrade. A railing incorporating a top rail supported by balusters (short, vertical members).

Batter. The inclination of a wall from the vertical.

Bay. The regularly repeated vertical sections that form the facade of a building.

Bracket. A member, affixed to a wall, that supports a projecting element above it.

Broken pediment. A pediment split at the apex, the void usually being filled with a decorative element such as an urn.

Cabochon. An escutcheonlike decoration with a round or oval convex surface at the center.

Cartouche. An ornamental frame, frequently decorated with elaborate scrolling and bearing an inscription or device in the central tablet.

Caryatids. Supporting elements, such as posts or pilasters, in the form of the human female figure.

Chamfer. A bevel at the edge of a masonry wall.

Channeling. Grooves cut into or between architectural members.

Chat sawing. A process in which zinc and lead ores are added in the sawing of masonry to create a mildly rough surface.

Cheek. A narrow upright element flanking the side of an architectural member such as a door.

Coffer. A deeply recessed panel in a ceiling.

Composite Order. See diagram.

Corbels. A series of stepped projections issuing from a wall, gradually extending farther horizontally in the higher courses; also, supporting projections.

Corbel table. A water table or stringcourse supported by corbels.

Corinthian Order. See diagram.

Cornice. See diagram.

Crenellation. Indented battlements.

Crocket. A Gothic ornament, usually in stylized plant form, that decorates vertical or sloping members.

Crossettes. Horizontal extensions of the moldings at the top of the frame of a door or window.

Cusping. In tracery, the intersection of two arcs.

Depressed arch. An arched opening in which the top is flattened.

Doric Order. See diagram.

Dormer. A window projecting from the slope of a roof.

Echinus. See diagram.

Engaged. Attached to a wall.

Entablature. See diagram.

Extrados. The outside curve of an arch.

Fenestration. The type of windows used in a building and their arrangement.

Festoon. A curved garland of plant and/or fruit forms.

Fillet. A narrow rectangular molding.

Fillet and torus. A narrow raised band with a projecting convex molding.

Finial. A decorative element capping a spire or pinnacle.

Fleuron. See diagram.

Flute. A channel running the length of a column or pilaster, also found in some moldings.

French Ionic. A variation of the Ionic Order in which the capitals are decorated with garlands.

Frieze. See diagram.

Gable. The triangular vertical section at the end of a double-sloped roof.

Guttae. See diagram.

Herm. A rectangular post or pillar topped by a bust.

Intrados. The inside curve of an arch.

Ionic Order. See diagram.

Keystone. The wedge-shaped stone at the top of an arch.

Lantern. A structure with windows on top of a roof.

Lintel. A horizontal member spanning an opening.

Lunette. A semicircular or crescent-shaped opening or window.

Machicolation. In medieval architecture, a projection atop a defensive wall.

Mansard. A roof with a double slope on each of four sides, the lower slope being steeper than the upper.

Metope. See diagram.

Modillion. A small horizontal bracket, usually scrolled, supporting the corona (see diagram) in the Corinthian and Composite Orders.

Mutule. See diagram.

Necking. See diagram.

Obelisk. A four-sided monolith, developed by the Egyptians, frequently used in architecture on a much smaller scale for decorative purposes.

Oculus. A round window or opening.

Ogive. A Gothic arch.

Order. In Classical architecture, a specific design and arrangement of column and entablature. See diagram.

Oriel. A window projecting from a wall; a bay window.

Palladian (Serlian) motif. A triple window or door, the central opening being arched, those adjacent being flat-headed.

Pediment. The triangular gable on a Classical building.

Pergola. An open colonnade, the columns frequently supporting beams only.

Pilaster. An engaged column or pier.

Porte cochere. A covered structure extending from the entrance to a building, intended to shelter people entering or leaving vehicles.

Portico. A covered colonnade, usually attached to the front of a building.

Pulvinated (frieze). Bulging out, pillow-shaped (see diagram).

Quoin. Members, usually of stone, that are used to mark the corner at which two walls meet.

Reveal. The part of a thick wall that frames a door or window.

Rinceau. A decorative element comprised of a symmetrical arrangement of swirling, stylized leaves.

Rock-face. Untreated stone surface used in masonry, or stone dressed to appear natural.

Roll molding. A rounded, cylindrical molding.

Rosette. A round floral decoration in relief.

Rostrum. A Classical decoration modeled after the prow of an ancient ship.

Rustication. Stonework in which the masonry is marked by channeling.

Scamozzi Ionic. A variation of the Ionic Order in which the capital's volutes radiate at 45°.

Soffit. The exposed underside of a spanning member, such as an arch or lintel.

Spandrel. The triangular area marked by the left or right extrados of an arch and the right angle that encloses it.

Springing. The point in an arch at which the support ends and the curve begins.

Stylobate. See diagram.

Swag. See festoon.

Triglyph. See diagram.

Tuscan (Florentine) arch. An arch in which the intrados is rounded and the extrados is pointed.

Tuscan Order. See diagram.

Vermiculated. Decorated by irregular, winding lines.

Vitruvian scroll. A Classical design of connected wavelike figures running in a band.

Volute. See diagram.

Voussoir. A wedge-shaped block in an arch.

Water table. A narrow band of masonry, running horizontally across a facade; also called a stringcourse.

DORIC ORDER

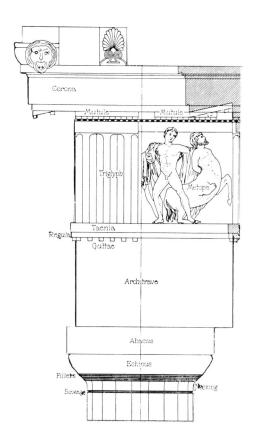

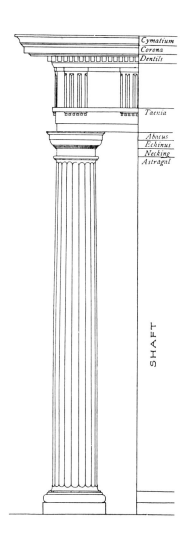

Cymatium
Corona
Dentils

Taenia

Abacus
Echinus
Necking
Astragal

SHAFT

IONIC ORDER

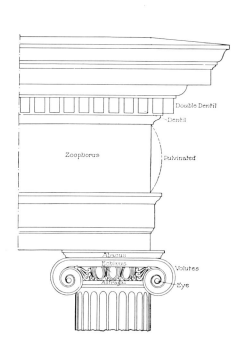

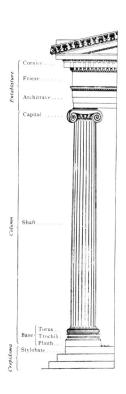

CORINTHIAN ORDER

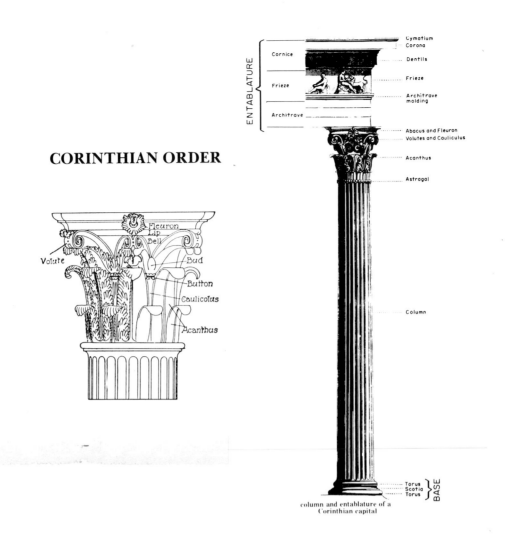

column and entablature of a
Corinthian capital

COMPOSITE ORDER

TUSCAN ORDER

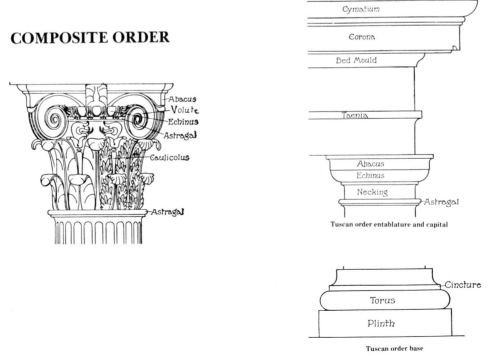

Tuscan order entablature and capital

Tuscan order base